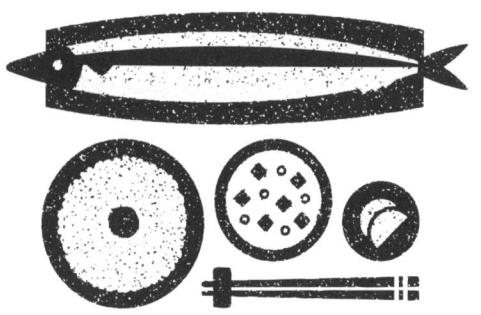

Japanese
Cooking
for Everyone
Motoko Kuroda

装　　幀＝寄藤文平　坂野達也
本文イラスト＝横井智美

日本の料理
Japanese Cooking
for Everyone

Motoko Kuroda
黒田基子＝著

はじめに

アメリカに住むようになって20年以上が過ぎました。何年たっても私の食生活の基本が日本食にあることは変わりませんが、限られた素材や家族や友人たちの好みによって、私のレパートリーはずいぶん変化してきました。

今や日本食は、アメリカ郊外のスーパーでもテイクアウトの寿司が普通に並んでいるほど一般的になりましたが、アメリカ人の日本食に対する好みは日本人とはちょっと違います。アメリカで子供を育て、アメリカ人を家に招いたりするうちに、意外な料理が好評だったり、逆に外国人好みだと思っていた料理が受けなかったりすることに気づきました。ただの豆ごはんやごま和えが絶賛されるかと思えば、手をかけた料理が不評ということもあります。

また、自宅やコミュニティーセンターで日本料理を教えることを通じて、日本食の基本を知らない人にとっては意外なことが難しいことも知りました。たとえば、おにぎりをほどよく握る感覚を、日ごろおにぎりを食べつけていない人に教えるのは不可能に近いのです。反面、ごはんをお鍋で炊くことを難しく考えるアメリカ人はほとんどいません。そもそも炊飯器というものが生活の

PREFACE

I have now been living in the United States for more than 20 years. While my basic diet has not changed from a Japanese one over the years, I have had to somewhat modify my repertoire due to limited ingredients and the tastes of my family and friends.

Japanese food, however, has now become so common in the United States that sushi can be found in the take-out sections of most suburban supermarkets, but Americans have slightly different tastes for it than the Japanese. I noticed, while raising my daughter and inviting Americans over for dinners and such, that they sometimes really liked some dishes that I presumed they would find odd, or were put off by some dishes that I thought would suit their Western tastes. Ordinary cooked rice with green peas or a simple dish with sesame dressing would be highly praised, while on occasion, dishes which I went to painstaking lengths to prepare would be ill-regarded.

I also discovered through my teaching of Japanese cooking at home, in community centers, and other places that for those uninitiated in the basics, some unexpected tasks could be difficult. For instance, I found it almost impossible to teach those who do not regularly eat *onigiri*, simple balls of rice, how to shape them with their hands. Americans who think it is difficult to cook

中にないので、米は鍋で調理するに決まっているからです。

　本書には、こうした経験を通じてアメリカ人に人気のあったレシピ、日本料理初心者でもつくれるレシピを集めました。中心になっているのは日本の基本料理ですが、伝統的なものとは限りません。子供に好評な料理、ベジタリアンがいても安心な料理も盛り込んであります。また、外国人に教える場合に必要だった素材や調理方法の解説も加えました。

　外国人、アメリカ人といってもさまざまですが、好まれる料理の基本は「シンプルであること」「わかりやすいこと」。これは家庭料理の基本でもあります。

　どのレシピもそのままの日本料理であるよりも、皆に喜ばれる実用的なものであること、限られた材料で簡単につくれることを念頭に置きました。

　本書を日本の家庭料理の入門書として、また外国人に日本料理を教える際の手引きとして活用していただければ幸いです。

2009年8月
黒田　基子

rice in a saucepan, however, are few and far between. That is because dedicated rice cookers are not normally found in a typical home, so cooking rice in a saucepan is the only option.

This book contains a collection of recipes based on these and other experiences. They are the recipes that were popular with Americans and are suitable for those who are just learning how to prepare Japanese food. The main focus is on basic Japanese recipes, but it is not limited to traditional ones. There are dishes that your kids will love, and dishes suited to vegetarians. I have also included explanations about the ingredients and cooking methods that were required when teaching foreigners.

People of all nationalities, just like Americans, have their individual differences, but the key to making enjoyable food is "simplicity and straightforwardness." This is also the foundation of home cooking.

Instead of making every recipe strictly Japanese, I have tried to make the recipes easy to follow using limited ingredients, so I hope they are useful and enjoyable for everyone.

This book is an introduction to Japanese home cooking, and it is my most sincere wish that it is also helpful when teaching foreigners and other people unfamiliar with our food how to prepare it.

August, 2009
Motoko Kuroda

目次

はじめに..4

1 まずごはんを炊こう..17

ごはんがなければ始まらない..18

日本人の子供も外国人の子供も大好き！
白いごはんはキッズフレンドリー 22

米の種類と扱い方..24

おいしいお米を手に入れるのが一番大切..28

米のとぎ方：「とぎ」が味を決める..32

お鍋でごはんを炊く：電気炊飯器がなくても大丈夫............38
● ごはんの炊き方 40

先入観がない外国人のほうが楽にお鍋でごはんを炊ける 42

ごはんの保存はお櫃と冷凍が最高..44

おにぎり：単純だけど難しい力加減..46
● 茶巾しぼりおにぎり 50 ● 具を入れる場合 50

ごはんもののバリエーション..50
● 豆ごはん 52 ● きのこごはん 54 ● 玄米 56

2 お寿司..61

誤解の多い日本料理の代表選手..62

酢飯のつくり方：おいしい酢飯が寿司の要..64
● 酢飯 66

Contents

PREFACE 5

1 Let's Cook Rice **17**

Nothing begins without cooked rice 19

All kids love rice.
White rice is the ultimate kid-friendly food 23

Rice varieties and how to handle them 25

Obtaining delicious rice is of utmost importance 29

Basic preparation—the art of *togu* 33

Cooking rice in a saucepan
—yes, you can cook rice without a rice cooker 39
• Cooking rice 41

Foreigners without any preconceptions can
cook rice easily in a saucepan 43

Preserving cooked rice—putting it in an *ohitsu*, a wooden
container meant for cooked rice, or the freezer, is best....45

***Onigiri*—they are simple,**
but applying just the right pressure is not easy..............47
• *Chakin-shibori onigiri* 51 • *Onigiri* with fillings 51

Rice variations 51
• *Mame-gohan* (rice with green peas) 53 • Rice with mushrooms 55
• Brown rice 57

2 Sushi **61**

The often-misunderstood Japanese champion 63

How to make sushi rice—it is essential for good sushi 65
• Sushi rice 67

簡単豪華な手巻き寿司 70
- カリフォルニアロールの手巻き 70

手巻きの具 76
- 魚 76 ● 野菜 80 ● 肉 82 ● 薬味類 82

寿司屋では食べられないちらし寿司 84
- 精進のちらし寿司 86 ● サケとイクラのちらし寿司 92

巻き寿司：ホームメイド寿司の上級編 94
- かっぱ巻き 96 ● 裏巻きのカリフォルニアロール 100

3 汁物いろいろ麺類いろいろ **105**

出汁は日本料理の万能選手 106
- かつお節と昆布の出汁 108 ● 煮干し出汁 108

かつお節と煮干し vs だしのもとやめんつゆ 110

汁物のバリエーション：
味噌味のもの、塩・醤油味のもの 114
- 味噌汁 114 ● 豚汁 116 ● お吸い物 120 ● かき玉汁 120
- けんちん汁 122

麺類のバリエーション 124
- 乾麺のゆで方 126 ● 冷たいそば（うどん）128
- 温かい汁そば（うどん）130

4 日本流野菜料理 **137**

切るだけの料理 138
- 早漬け 138 ● 醤油漬け 142 ● きゅうりもみ 142 ● 大根おろし 144

Simple yet deluxe hand-rolled sushi..............................71
- Hand-rolled california rolls 71

Other ingredients that can be used as fillings for hand-rolled sushi 77
- Fish 77 • Vegetables 81 • Meat 83 • Condiments 83

***Chirashi-zushi* (literally, "scattered sushi") —not available at sushi restaurants**.............................85
- A purist's approach to *chirashi-zushi* 87
- *Chirashi-zushi* with salmon and salmon roe 93

Sushi rolls—advanced home-made sushi 95
- *Kappa-maki* (cucumber roll) 97 • Inside-out California rolls 101

3 Soups and Noodles, Oodles and Oodles 105

***Dashi*—Japan's all-around player** 107
Bonito flake and *konbu dashi* 109 • Dried sardine *dashi* 109

Bonito flake and dried sardine *dashi* vs. instant *dashi* and prepared noodle broth 111

Soup variations—they come in *miso* and salt/ soy sauce flavors 115
- *Miso* soup 115 • *Tonjiru* (pork and vegetable soup) 117
- *Osuimono* (clear soups) 121 • Eggdrop soup 121
- *Kenchin* soup 123

Variations using noodles..125
- Cooking dried noodles 127 • Cold *soba* (or *udon*) 129
- *Soba* (or *udon*) in a hot soup 131

4 Cooking with Vegetables—Japanese-Style 137

Just-cut cooking 139
- *Haya-zuke* (quick pickling) 139
- *Shoyu-zuke* (pickling in soy sauce) 143
- *Kyuri-momi* (cucumbers in a vinegar dressing) 143
- Grated *daikon* 145

| 包丁修行は「ネコの手」から | 144 |
| ゆでたり煮たり | 146 |

- おひたし 148 • ごま和え 150

| 急成長中の枝豆人気 | 152 |
| 焼き野菜料理 | 154 |

- 焼きなす 154 • きのこホイル焼き 156 • 根菜のオーブン焼き 158

| 炒めて煮る | 160 |

- きんぴらごぼう 160 • セロリきんぴら 164 • ピーマンきんぴら 164

| 揚げ野菜 | 166 |

- 精進揚げ 166 • れんこん肉詰め 170

5　豆腐には味がある　　175

日本伝統の健康食	176
ヘルシーだけど味がない、という誤解	176
豆腐そのものを味わう料理	178

- 冷奴 178 • 湯豆腐 180 • 田楽 182 • 練り味噌バリエーション 186
- 油揚げの素焼き 188

| 最近はやりのグルメ系豆腐は初心者にもわかる濃厚な旨味 | 190 |
| しっかり味つけした豆腐料理 | 190 |

- 肉豆腐 192 • マーボー豆腐 192

| ちょっと手のかかった豆腐料理 | 196 |

- 白和え 196

Knife training begins with "the paw of the cat"............145

Boiling and simmering..147
- *Ohitashi* 149 • Sesame dressing 151

***Edamame*—they are taking the United States by storm** ...153

Grilled vegetables 155
- Grilled eggplant 155 • Mushrooms grilled in foil 157
- Baked root vegetables 159

***Kinpira* (saute and simmer) technique** 161
- Sauteed and simmered burdock root 161
- Sauteed and simmered celery 165
- Sauteed and simmered green peppers 165

Deep-fried vegetables..167
- Vegetable tempura 167 • Lotus root stuffed with meat 171

5 Tofu—It Has Taste **175**

Japan's traditional health food 177

It is healthy, but tasteless—the misconception............177

Recipes for enjoying the taste of tofu..........................179
- Chilled tofu with toppings 179 • Simmered tofu 181
- *Dengaku* (tofu coated in a *miso* sauce and grilled) 183
- Prepared *miso*—variations 187
- Grilled *aburaage* (regular tofu that has been cut in thin slices and deep fried) 189

Gourmet tofu—gaining in popularity, even beginners can appreciate its rich taste..191

Full-flavored tofu dishes 191
- Braised meat and tofu 193 • Mapo tofu 193

High-maintenance tofu 197
- *Shira-ae* (mashed tofu salad) 197

6 肉、魚、卵のおかず..**201**

魚は日本の健康食..202
- 照り焼き 202 • 味噌漬け 204 • 味噌焼き 206 • たたき 208
- 天ぷら 210 • ホイル焼き 214

醤油や味噌で肉をおいしく..........................216
- 照り焼き 216 • 焼き鳥 218 • とんかつ 220 • しょうが焼き 224
- つくね 226 • エビ入りつくね 228 • そぼろごはん 230
- 唐揚げ 232

やさしい味の卵料理......................................234
- 卵焼き 234 • 親子どんぶり 238

7 便利な調味料やスパイスの使い方..............**243**

醤油..244

味噌..246

酒..248

みりん..250

だしのもと・めんつゆ..................................250

海藻類..252

かつお節..254

ポン酢..254

すし酢..256

わさび..256

日本の野菜..258
- しそ 258 • ねぎ、わけぎ 258

---

*本書の作り方は4人分を目安にしています。
*計量表記は以下を基準にしています。
　1カップ = 200mℓ　大さじ1 = 15mℓ　小さじ1 = 5mℓ

6 Meat, Fish, and Eggs **201**

Fish—Japan's health food 203
- Teriyaki 203 • *Miso* marinade 205 • *Misoyaki* 207
- *Tataki* (briefly seared fish) 209 • Tempura 211 • Foil wraps 215

Soy sauce and *miso* marinades for meat 217
- Teriyaki 217 • *Yakitori* 219
- *Tonkatsu* (breaded, deep-fried pork cutlets) 221 • Ginger pork 225
- *Tsukune* (Japanese chicken meatballs) 227
- *Tsukune* (chicken meatball) with shrimp 229
- Ground chicken and egg with rice 231 • Japanese fried chicken 233

A light and fluffy egg dish 235
- *Tamago-yaki* (a Japanese-style omelet) 235
- *Oyako donburi* (chicken and egg on rice) 239

7 Convenient Seasonings—How to Use Them ... **243**

Soy sauce 245

Miso 247

Sake 249

Mirin 251

Instant *dashi* (soup stock) granules and noodle broths 251

Seaweed 253

Dried bonito flakes 255

Ponzu 255

Sushi vinegar 257

Wasabi 257

Japanese vegetables 259
- *Shiso* 259 • *Negi* and *Wakegi* 259

---

* Recipes in this book are designed to serve roughly 4 persons.
* Measures indicated may be converted as follows:
   1 cup = 200 mℓ   1 tablespoon = 15 mℓ   1 teaspoon = 5 mℓ

1

まずごはんを炊こう
Let's Cook Rice

ごはんがなければ始まらない

1 まずごはんを炊こう

　ごはんの支度の際、日本人がまず最初にとりかかるのはお米をといでしかけることです。朝ごはんやお弁当のために、前の晩に炊飯器にお米をセットしておく方も多いでしょう。今日はちょっと遅くなる、というとき、家にいる子供に「お米だけといでおいてね」というのもよくあること。ごはんさえ炊けていればまずは安心、という感覚は、日本人ならたいていは持っているものです。

　それは、日本人には「ごはんが主食、おかずが副食」という考え方があるから。和食ではごはんが主食だから、洋食ではパンが主食、と考えたくなりますが、主食・副食という考え方そのものが、実はとても日本的です。

　たとえば、アメリカでレストランに入ると、まずパンとバター、またはオリーブオイル（最近の流行です）が出てきます。主食というよりは前菜というか、食事前におなかをなだめるスナックという感じです。たいていのアメリカ人がパンを食べるのは注文した料理が出てくるまでで、そのあとはほとんどパンには手をつけません。食事には必ずパンがなければ、という感覚はないのです。家庭でのディナーにはパンもごはんも出ないことも珍しくありません。

　ですから、外国人に日本人のお米のごはんに対する思い入れを説明するのはちょっと難しいのです。とはいえ、おいしいものは誰が食べてもおいしいので、よく炊

Nothing begins without cooked rice

The first thing we do when preparing a meal is to make rice. Many of us might do this the night before in preperation for the day's breakfast or boxed lunch. Often, when we know we will be coming home late, we tell our children at home to at least prepare the rice. Most Japanese feel secure knowing that at least the rice has been cooked.

For we Japanese, rice is the staple of our diet, and all the other dishes are merely an accompaniment. We actually like to think that, since rice is the staple of our diet, bread must be the staple of a Western-style dinner. But, in actuality, the very idea of a "staple" and other "accompaniments" is very Japanese in itself.

For instance, when you go to a restaurant in the United States, bread is first served with butter or olive oil (the latter being a recent trend). It is actually more of an appetizer—a light snack to keep our stomachs from growling before the meal arrives. Most Americans munch on their bread until what they have ordered arrives, and then hardly ever touch it again. There is no feeling that there has to be bread for it to be a meal. It is not unusual for there to be neither bread nor rice served during a meal at home.

That is why it is so difficult to explain to foreigners why we have such a considerable fondness for our rice. But, then again, delicious things are delicious to

けたごはんは外国人も好んで食べてくれます。そして、このライスは自分たちが普段食べているものよりおいしいけど、どうやってつくるのか、と聞かれることもよくあります。

日本食はなんといってもお米が基本。私は日本食のつくり方を外国人に教えるときには、生徒が大人でも子供でも、米の選び方とごはんの炊き方から始めます。日本人にとっては常識でも、一から説明しなければいけないことがたくさんあります。お米は、種類によって味やねばりが違うので、ローンググレインライス（いわゆる外米）でなく、ミディアムグレインライス（うるち米）を買ってこなければ日本風のごはんは炊けない、というところから話が始まります。

寿司がすっかりアメリカで市民権を得た昨今では、日本風のごはんそのものはよく知られています。が、寿司のライスがアメリカの米のようにパラパラにならないのは、炊き方やまぜ込む酢に秘密があるのだ、と思い込んでいるアメリカ人も珍しくありません。米の種類の違いから始まって、上等の新米コシヒカリと去年の無ブランド米がどうしてこんなにも値段が違うのか、というところまで話がたどり着くにはかなり根気がいりますが、正しいお米の選び方とおいしいごはんの炊き方を理解できれば、日本食のつくり方を半分はマスターできたようなものです。

everyone, so foreigners are quite happy eating rice that has been properly cooked. And, because it is tastier than what they have had before, I am often asked how to make it.

Rice, without a doubt, is the very foundation of Japanese food. When I teach foreigners how to prepare Japanese food, whether they are adults or kids, I first teach them how to select and cook rice. From the Japanese perspective, even if it seems like common knowledge, we feel that there are many things we have to teach from the beginning. The taste, stickiness, and other qualities of rice differ from one variety to another, so it is important to choose medium-grain rice, not long-grain rice, which we refer to as "foreign rice." Without the right variety of rice, you will not be able to cook it Japanese-style, and that is where we begin.

In recent years sushi has become an honorary U.S. citizen, and Japanese-style rice itself has become quite well known. But it is not unusual to find Americans who are convinced that sushi rice sticks together nicely while American rice does not simply because of the way it is cooked, the addition of vinegar, and other such "secrets." It all starts with the variety of rice. It takes a fair amount of patience to delve deeply into the subject. Why, for instance, is this year's *koshihikari* rice so much more expensive than last year's no-name brand? But, if you can learn how to choose the right rice, and how to cook it, you have probably come halfway to mastering the art of Japanese cooking.

日本人の子供も外国人の子供も大好き！
白いごはんはキッズフレンドリー

1 まずごはんを炊こう

　どんなに好き嫌いが激しい子供でも、白いごはんが嫌いという子供は日本では聞いたことがありません。ふりかけごはんや味噌汁かけごはんが嫌いな子供はまずいないでしょう。味噌汁かけごはんはともかく、白いごはんはアメリカの子供も大好き。平均的なアメリカの子供の偏食ぶりは日本の子供の比ではありませんが、白いごはんを食べない子供はほとんどいません。食べられるものを数えたほうが早いような子でも、白いごはんを出すと喜んで食べることがほとんどです。

　アメリカで、娘が通う幼稚園や学校にごはんを持っていったり、おにぎりのつくり方を教えたりしたときも、いつでも白いごはんは好評でした。おにぎりといっても海苔(のり)は巻かず、中には何もいれません。ほんとうに素のままのライスボール。ポイントは小細工をしないこと。日本のお子様ランチや幼稚園弁当の感覚でいろいろ盛り合わせると、警戒して食べてくれなくなります。愛想も素っ気もない白いごはんをお皿にのせただけというのがいいのです。そのわかりやすさこそごはんの要。そこに、子供によってはお醤油(しょうゆ)をかけます（中華料理のテイクアウトが日常化しているので、醤油味はアメリカの子供にもなじみがあります）。塩も出しておきますが、圧倒的に醤油が人気。これは大人もよくやります。

All kids love rice. White rice is the ultimate kid-friendly food

I have never heard of even the pickiest kids in Japan disliking white rice. Certainly no kid dislikes rice if it has a sprinkle of flavorful *furikake* or a splash of *miso* soup on it. Okay, setting aside the bowl of rice with *miso* soup poured over it, American kids love white rice, too. Without comparing the fussy eating habits of the average American kid to those of Japanese kids, it is safe to say that very few American kids cannot tolerate white rice. Even most really troublesome kids, the ones where you count what they like rather than what they dislike because it is easier, are overjoyed when the white rice is served and gobble it down.

In the United States, when I took rice to my daughter's school for her classmates and taught them how to make *onigiri*, white rice was always a favorite. We would never wrap the *onigiri* with sheets of *nori* (seaweed), nor put anything inside of them. They were rice balls in their purest form. The trick to making them is to avoid cheap tricks altogether. Kids get suspicious and will not eat the Japanese standard "kid's lunch" or kindergarten box lunch that has too many different items all grouped together. Plain white rice, served matter-of-factly on a plate, is perfectly fine. The key is the very simplicity of rice. Some kids in the United States put soy sauce on their rice (they have developed a taste for soy sauce

寿司の影響か、ごはんには醤油と思い込んでいるアメリカ人はかなりいます。「ごはんが主食、おかずが副食」という考え方がないので、アメリカ人はおかずを食べながらごはんを食べるということをしません。おかずはおかずだけ、ごはんはごはんだけ食べる。だからごはんだけだと味がない。したがって醤油をかける、というわけです。日本人から見ると恐ろしくなるほどたっぷりと醤油をかけている場合もありますが、毎日食べるわけではなし、本人がおいしければそれでよしとしましょう。

米の種類と扱い方

おいしい日本のごはんを炊くには、まず、正しい種類の米を買ってくることが第一歩。お米の種類の説明から始めましょう。

日本の米の分類は、うるち米ともち米。うるち米は、さらにジャポニカ種（日本の一般的な米）とインディカ種（粘り気のない、いわゆる外米）に分類されます。が、外国人には、長粒米（外米）、中粒米（日本のうるち米）、短粒米（もち米）の3種類として説明したほうが、見た目からもわかりやすいと思います。粒が短いほど澱粉質が多くなるので、その分粘り気が増します。

because Chinese take-out food has become so common). Salt is also on the table, but they almost always go for the soy sauce. Adults are much the same.

Perhaps it is the influence of sushi, but many Americans are convinced that soy sauce goes with rice. Because they do not have the same concept that rice is the staple and other dishes merely accompaniments, Americans do not eat accompaniments along with their rice. If they eat other dishes, they eat only those other dishes; when they eat rice, they eat only rice. That is why they think rice alone is tasteless. It follows that they put soy sauce on their rice. From the Japanese perspective, at times it is frightening how they drown their rice with soy sauce, but since they do not eat it like that every day, we can forgive them as long as they enjoy it.

Rice varieties and how to handle them

If you are going to cook delicious Japanese rice, then the first step is to buy the right variety. Let me begin by explaining a bit about rice varieties.

Japanese rice can be divided broadly into non-glutinous and glutinous (sticky) rice. Non-glutinous rice, or ordinary rice, can be further divided. There is *japonica*, the normal variety that we use, and *indica*, which is much less sticky and which we refer to as "foreign rice." But, for foreigners, I prefer to divide rice into three types, as the differences are clearly visible with the

1 まずごはんを炊こう

　日本国内であれば、米はブランドこそ豊富ですが、店頭に並んでいるほとんどがうるち米。もち米や玄米でさえなければ、どれを使っても同じ炊き方で日本のごはんができるわけですが、外国ではそうはいきません。欧米のスーパーで一般的に売られているのは長粒米が中心ですが、最近のグルメブームで、アメリカのグルメ食材店や自然食品店には驚くほど多様な米が並んでいます。長粒米だけでも、アメリカ米に限らずインドのバスマティライスやタイのジャスミンライス（香り米）など、ちょっと気のきいたスーパーなら置いてあります。

　日本風のうるち米は中粒米に分類される場合も短粒米に分類される場合もありますが、もち米と比べると明らかに長いので、区別するためには中粒米と考えたほうがわかりやすいかもしれません。アメリカでは「すしライス」という名称で販売されていたりします。「スティッキーライス（粘りのある米）」と呼ぶ人もいますが、もち米と混同されやすいのでこう呼ぶのはおすすめしません。中粒米としては、ほかにイタリアのアルボリオライス（リゾット用の米）も知られています。こうした何種類もの米それぞれに、玄米や有機米などのバリエーションがあります。

　英語でブラウンライスと呼ばれる玄米は、精米前のぬかや胚芽を含む米。栄養も繊維質も豊富ですが、炊き方

eye: long-grain, medium-grain (Japanese), and short-grain (glutinous). The shorter the rice grain, the greater the starch content, and the stickier the rice.

Within Japan there are a multitude of rice brands, but almost all the rice displayed on store shelves is Japanese medium-grain rice. If it were not for the presence of some glutinous rice and brown rice, then I could say all rice in Japan can be cooked in the same manner, but that is not the case outside of Japan. In the West, long-grain rice takes center stage at the supermarket. But, go to a gourmet food store, the product of the recent gourmet boom in the United States, or any health food store, and you will find an amazing number of varieties of rice on the shelves. Even for long-grain rice, a decent supermarket will display more than just American; you will find Indian Basmati rice, Thai Jasmine (aromatic) rice, and others.

Japanese-style rice is sometimes classified as medium-grain, sometimes classified as short-grain. I think it is easier to think of it as medium-grain, because it is obviously longer than glutinous (sticky) rice. Sometimes it is labeled "sushi rice" in the United States. Some people even refer to it as "sticky rice," but I do not recommend such naming as it is easy to mix it up with glutinous rice. In addition to Japanese-style rice, Italian Arborio rice (used in risotto) is also a medium-grain rice that is well known. All of these types of rice are available in various brown and organic versions.

What is known in English as brown rice is the hulled rice prior to any further milling steps which

も食感も白米とは異なるので、とりあえずは白米から始めましょう。胚芽米は玄米から表皮ぬか層だけをとり除いて胚芽部分を残したお米です。栄養価の面からは玄米と白米の中間ということになります。炊き方は白米と同じで味わいも近いので、白米のレシピはいずれも胚芽米にも使えます。ただし、海外では胚芽米というジャンルは知られていないので、日本食料品店でないと入手できません。

おいしいお米を手に入れるのが一番大切

　初めて日本のお米を買いに行くアメリカ人には、私は「お米の値段はワインと同じ」と教えます。基本的には高いほどおいしいけれど、例外もあれば好みにもよります。アメリカでは米の種類こそ豊富に出回っていますが、ブランド米などという概念はありません。さらに新米・古米という感覚もまずありません。ブランドによって値段が倍にも3倍にもなることも、新米が出回るころになると去年のお米がセール価格になることも、実際に味わって経験しているわけではないのでピンとこないのです。

remove the bran and germ. It is more nutritious and contains a lot of fiber, but the way it is cooked and its texture differ from white rice, so let me begin with white rice. *Haiga* rice is rice that has had its layer of bran removed but retains the germ. It is between brown rice and white rice in terms of nutritional value. It is cooked the same way as white rice and the taste is quite similar, so, *haiga* rice can be used in any of the recipes calling for white rice. However, *haiga* rice is not well known overseas, so it would be easiest to obtain it at a shop specializing in Japanese foods.

Obtaining delicious rice is of utmost importance

I explain to Americans setting off to buy Japanese rice for the first time that, in terms of price, buying rice is much like buying a bottle of wine. It is basically true that the more expensive it is, the more delicious, but there are exceptions, and it depends somewhat on your taste. While there are many varieties of rice on store shelves in the United States, Americans are not very brand conscious. And, when it comes to new rice and old rice, there is no consciousness at all. Some brands may be double or triple the price of others, and when the new rice begins to circulate, last year's rice goes on sale. But if you have not tasted the difference, then it is hard to comprehend.

ブランドはともかくとして、海外で米を購入する場合、鮮度を見極めることは大切です。ポイントはとにかく商品の回転のよい店で買うこと。日本食料品店やアジア食品店が近くにあれば一番確実ですが、ない場合は繁盛しているグルメ食料品店や自然食品店で購入することをおすすめします。時間とともに精米後の米の味が急速に落ちていくことは日本では常識ですが、アメリカでは売るほうも買うほうも、生米の鮮度を気にする人はめったにいません。日本では考えられないほど長期間たなざらしになっている米もありますから、要注意です。

　気をつけて購入すれば、海外の米も捨てたものではありません。アメリカのカリフォルニア米は日本の米と遜色ないほどおいしいですし、その上安いのもうれしいところ。ブランドもかなりたくさんあるので、好みに合わせて選べます。また、玄米に関しては日本より種類が豊富です。特におすすめは日本ではあまり見かけないもち米の玄米。粘り気のある分、しっとりしていて、うるち米の玄米よりおいしいと思います。

Setting aside the issue of brands, when buying rice overseas, it is important to establish its freshness. You should buy from a retail outlet with good turnover. If you have a store specializing in Japanese foods nearby, or an Asian foods store, then that is a safe bet, but otherwise you should look for a busy gourmet or natural foods store. That the taste of rice will deteriorate quickly after milling is common knowledge in Japan, but in the United States you will rarely come across anyone concerned about rice's freshness, whether they are buying or selling. From a Japanese perspective, it is unbelievable how long some of the rice sold in the United States has been gathering dust on supermarket shelves, so please exercise caution.

There is nothing wrong with rice that has been purchased overseas if it has been chosen with care. Californian rice is right up there with Japanese rice in terms of taste, and it is great that it is so inexpensive. There are also many brands, so you can choose the one you like best. And, when it comes to brown rice, there are many more varieties available in the United States than in Japan. In particular, I would like to recommend brown glutinous rice, which is very difficult to find in Japan. It is sticky, yet moist; I think it tastes better than ordinary brown rice.

米のとぎ方：「とぎ」が味を決める

1 まずごはんを炊こう

　おいしいごはんを炊くにはお米をきちんと「とぐ」ことが何よりも大切です。「米はとげばとぐほどおいしくなる」といってもいいでしょう。ただし、米が余計な水分を吸わないうちに手早くとぐことも大切です。私は、いつも最初に、「米に水を入れたら、電話が鳴ろうが何が起ころうが、決して中断せずにとぎ続けること」と大げさなくらい念を押します。

　最近は無洗米も出回っていますが、無洗米でもといだほうがおいしくなります。ずいぶん前のことになりますが、アメリカで販売されている米（日本風のうるち米）のパッケージに、無洗米でもないのに「洗ってはいけない」と書いてあるのを発見したことがあります。栄養価を考えてのことなのかもしれませんが、パッケージに書いてあるつくり方には油断がなりません。正しいつくり方を書いてある場合もあるのでしょうが、以来「パッケージのつくり方は信用しないで、私の言うことを聞きなさい」と言うことにしています。

　さて、「とぎ」ですが、この「とぐ」ということを説明するのがなかなか厄介です。正確に翻訳できる英語がないので、washとかscrubを使うことになりますが、いずれにしてもピンときません。「米を洗って」と言ったら「洗剤は入れなくていいのか？」と聞かれたことがあります。食品を洗うのに洗剤は使いませんが、野菜の農

Basic preparation—the art of *togu*

You have to *togu* (a verb) the rice properly if you want to savor delicious rice. In fact, it is more important than any other preparation step. You could say, "the more you *togu* it, the more delicious the rice." To *togu* means to wash and rinse the rice, but I will explain more about that later. My policy is that once the rice comes in contact with water, I continue to *togu* whether the phone rings or anything else happens. Okay, I realize that is a bit extreme.

These days *musenmai*, or "no-washing-necessary" rice is available. Actually, *musenmai* tastes better if you *togu* it. Now, this may go back quite a while, but there was a time in the United States when I discovered written on a package of Japanese rice, even though it was not actually *musenmai*, "Do Not Wash." They might have been trying to conserve the nutritional value, but, anyway, you have to be careful about the directions you read on the backs of packages. There are cases when what is written on the package is correct, but there were numerous times in the past that I told students to ignore what was written on the package and "just do as I say!"

Okay, it is time to explain exactly what *togu* means. It is actually more difficult to explain than you would think, though. There really is no exact English translation, so "wash" and "scrub" are often used, but neither is quite right. If you choose to use "wash," then one wonders if a bit of detergent should be added. I have ac-

薬を落とすために専用の洗剤を使う場合もあります。でも、米をとぐのは清潔にするためや農薬を落とすためではありません。

「とぐ」の意味を明確にするためには、まず「とぐ」のは何のためかを説明しましょう。米をとぐのは精米後も付着している余分な糠（ぬか）を洗い流して雑味をとり除くためです。とぐことによって栄養分も減ることにはなりますが、味はぐんとよくなります。私は、アップルパイのリンゴの皮をむいたり、マッシュポテトのじゃがいもの皮をむくのと同じ、と説明しています。皮には繊維質や栄養が豊富ですが、だからといって皮ごとつぶしたら滑らかなマッシュポテトはできません。また、皮ごと食べておいしい料理もありますが、それはそれで別のもの。お米も、玄米はそれなりにおいしいものですが、白米はしっかりとがなければおいしく炊けません。

鍋かボウルに米とたっぷりの水を入れたらザッとかきまぜて、水を流します。ここはなるべく手早くします。水はほんの少し残します。米を軽くつかんで手を手前に引き、そのまま手のひらを押し出して押し出して米をとぎます。ここで力任せにごしごしやると米が割れるので、それなりの力加減を目で見て覚えてもらいます。手を使いたくない場合には泡立て器を使ってもかまいません。むしろ最初から泡立て器を使って教えたほうがわかりやすいかもしれません。私は子供に教える場合には泡立て器を使います。

tually been asked that. Detergent is never used to wash food, but there are occasions when a special kind of cleanser is used to remove agricultural chemicals from vegetables. Actually, neither "cleansing" nor "removing agricultural chemicals" is at the heart of the matter.

In order to get to the heart of the meaning of *togu*, let me explain why we do it. To *togu* is to remove the bran that is leftover from the milling process; the bran is an unintentional extra flavor. When you *togu* your rice, it loses some of its nutritional value, but the taste improves by leaps and bounds. I try to explain that it is similar to removing the skins of apples when making apple pie, or peeling potatoes when you make mashed potatoes. Skins have fiber and other nutritional value, but who can make smooth mashed potatoes when you have to crush up the skins? Of course, there are some foods that taste better with the skin, but that is another subject. As for rice, brown rice is wonderful in its own way, but white rice takes diligence when it comes to cooking it so that the taste is just right.

Add plenty of water to a saucepan or a bowl containing rice. Swish the rice around briefly then drain. Do this as quickly as possible, leaving just a little bit of water behind. Then, without adding more water, rub the rice against the bottom of the bowl using the palm of one hand. If you push down too hard, as if you were kneading bread, you will break the grains, so it is best to learn by watching someone who knows how to apply just the right amount of pressure. You can also use a whisk if you do not want to use your hand. In fact, if

ある程度といだら、再び水をたっぷり入れて流します。この後、水を入れては軽くまぜて流すことを、水が澄んでくるまで繰り返します。3、4回は必要でしょう。そして、最後にしっかりと水を切ります。私は、外国人に教えるときはザルを使って水を切るようにしています。途中で水を流すときにも、上澄みだけをうまく流すことができない場合にはザルを使います。これも、子供に教えるときには、最初からザルです。ちょっと時間がかかりますが仕方ありません。うっかりするととぎあとに米を計量し直さなければならないほど減ってしまうこともありますから。

① ボウルに米とたっぷりの水を入れる

② ザッとかきまぜ 水を流す
(①②は、なるべく手早くする)

③ 米を軽くつかんで手を手前に引き、そのまま手のひらを押し出して米をとぐ
(ゴシゴシ力を入れない)

泡立て器を使ってもよい

1. Place rice in a bowl and fill with plenty of water.
2. Mix quickly with your hand then pour out the water. (Complete steps 1 and 2 as quickly as possible)
3. Gently pull a handful of rice towards you and then push down with the palm of your hand. (Do not apply too much pressure.) A whisk works well, too.

you are teaching, it is probably easiest to start with a whisk. I use a whisk when I teach kids.

After rubbing the grains together with the palm of your hand for a while, add plenty of water and drain. After this, add water again, gently swish the rice around, and drain. Continue doing this until the water becomes clear, about 3 or 4 times. The last step is to completely drain the rice. When I teach foreigners, I drain the rice in a strainer. There are some people who are just not able to decanter the water off when draining. When this happens, I have them use a strainer. That goes for kids, too, from the beginning. It takes a bit more time, but there really is no choice. If you are not careful, they will lose so much rice by the time they finish washing it that you need to put it back in the measuring cup to gauge what has been lost.

---

4. After doing this several times, fill the bowl with plenty of water; pour out the water. Repeat 3 or 4 times until the water is clear.
5. When clear, pour out every last drop of water.

* You will not lose any rice if you use a sieve for steps 4 and 5.

お鍋でごはんを炊く：
電気炊飯器がなくても大丈夫

1 まずごはんを炊こう

　日本ではほとんどの家庭に自動炊飯器があります。炊飯器さえあれば、お米をといだあとは、目盛りどおりに水加減をしてスイッチを押すだけです。が、当然のことながら欧米の家庭に炊飯器はまずありませんから、ごはんは鍋で炊くしかありません。スイッチ1つのやり方に慣れていると面倒に感じるかもしれませんが、やってみると意外に簡単なものです。ただ、これにはいくつか注意がいります。

　まず、お米の量ですが、1回に炊けるのは3カップが上限です。炊飯器や昔風のかまどで炊く場合には、下からばかりでなく脇からも熱があたりますが、鍋で炊く場合、熱は下からしかあたりません。そのため、大量だとむらができてうまく炊けないのです。量が少ない分には1合でも大丈夫です。

　次に鍋ですが、これは熱回りが均等になるように厚手のしっかりしたものが必要です。日本では土鍋を使うことも多いですが、土鍋のように底に丸みのあるものは欧米に多い電熱レンジには向きません。炎の出るガスレンジと違って、鍋が直接触れないと熱が伝導しない電熱レンジでは底が平たい鍋がいいのです。深さのあまりない寸胴(ずんどう)な鍋で、ぴっちりと閉まる蓋(ふた)のあるものが最適です。

Cooking rice in a saucepan—yes, you can cook rice without a rice cooker

Almost every home in Japan has an automatic rice cooker. If you have a rice cooker, you simply put the washed rice in it, add water to the right mark, and press the "cook" button. But it almost goes without saying that rice cookers cannot be found in kitchens in the West, so there is no alternative to cooking it in a saucepan. If you are used to just pressing one button, then it may seem a bit troublesome at first, but you will soon find that it is surprisingly easy. You do, however, need to be careful about a few things.

First, regarding the amount of rice, 3 cups is the maximum you can cook at one time. Rice cookers and the old fashioned kiln-like *kamado* are heated from the sides as well as the bottom, whereas the heat only comes from the bottom on a stovetop, so too much rice will result in unevenly cooked rice. When you do not need a lot of rice, you can cook as little as 1 cup at a time.

For the saucepan, you need a good, thick-bottomed one that heats evenly. Earthen pots are often used in Japan, but earthen pots, with their rounded bottoms, are not suited to the electric ranges so common in the West. Unlike when using a gas flame, the bottom of the saucepan must be in contact with the heating element, so a flat-bottomed saucepan is most suitable. A straightt-sided saucepan that is not too deep and has a

ここに書いた火の加減や炊き上がる時間は、目安です。レンジによって異なるので、最初は目を離さずに火加減を調節するようにします。ある程度慣れれば、ちょうどいい時間にタイマーをセットしておくだけで大丈夫です。途中でこまめに火加減を調節する必要はありません。

ごはんの炊き方

米 ………… 2カップ
水 ………… 2カップ～ 2¼カップ（好みで調節する）

1. 鍋に米と水を入れ、米をこすり合わせるようにしてとぐ。何度も水をかえて水が透き通ってくるまで洗い流す。
2. 水を加え、20分以上そのまま置く（水の計量は正確にし、水が米に均一にかぶるように注意する）。
3. 蓋をして、弱めの中火で炊く（約15分）。火にかけたあとは、途中でまぜたり、蓋をあけたりしないこと。途中でふきこぼれそうになったら火を弱める。水がすっかり吸収されたら火を止めて、そのまま10分程度蒸らす（蓋はしたまま）。

＊水の量は、ごはんの硬さの好みとお米の状態によって加減します。特に新米の場合には、米が水分を多く含んでいるので、少なめの水で炊きます。

tight-fitting lid is perfect for the job.

The heat levels and cooking times mentioned here are only a guideline. They vary from stove to stove, so keep an eye on the rice and adjust the heat accordingly. After you get used to cooking rice on the stove, you will be able to set a timer to it. You do not have to keep adjusting the heat while the rice is cooking.

Cooking rice

2 cups rice
2 to 2¼ cups water (adjust to taste)

1. Place rice in saucepan. Wash and drain repeatedly until water is clear; drain completely.
2. Add water and let soak for at least 20 minutes (measure water carefully and make sure it covers the rice evenly).
3. Cover and cook at medium-low (about 15 minutes). After heating, do not stir rice or remove the cover. If it looks like it will spill over, lower the heat. When the water is fully absorbed, turn off the heat; let stand, covered, 10 minutes.

* The amount of water should be adjusted depending on how firm you like your rice and the condition of the rice itself. The moisture content of new rice, in particular, is higher, so less water is needed.

先入観がない外国人のほうが楽にお鍋でごはんを炊ける

現代の日本人の多くは、物心ついたときから家に電気炊飯器があった世代です。お鍋でごはんを炊いたことが1回もない日本人も珍しくないと思います。ですから、鍋でごはんを炊くというだけで、ちょっとしり込みしてしまう人も多いようです。20年前にアメリカに来たころは、私もごはんは炊飯器で炊くものと思い込んでいました。アパートで一人暮らしを始めたときも、まず第一に小さな炊飯器を必需品として購入しました。でも、その炊飯器が壊れたときに、鍋で炊いてみたところ意外に簡単だったのです。しかも安物の炊飯器で炊くよりよほどおいしく炊けました。そうなると、狭いアパートのキッチンに単機能でかさばる炊飯器を置くスペースが惜しくなり、以来炊飯器は使っていません。

だいたいアメリカのキッチンには炊飯器などなくて当然ですから、日本食を初めてつくるアメリカ人は、誰も鍋でお米を炊くことを恐れたりしません。そして、レシピどおりにすれば子供でもちゃんとごはんが炊けます。

近所の子供たちにお料理を教えていたころ、1回だけ生徒の1人からSOSの電話をもらったことがあります。その子は8カップものお米を大鍋で一度に炊こうとしたのです。一度に炊ける量は3カップまでと言ってあるのに、そこは子供のことで、パーティーのために張り切ってたくさん炊こうとしたらしいのです。様子を見に行っ

Foreigners without any preconceptions can cook rice easily in a saucepan

Most present-day Japanese have had electric rice cookers in their homes since they can first remember. It is not unusual for a Japanese to have never cooked rice in a saucepan, so a lot of Japanese seem a bit hesitant about the idea. When I first came to the United States 20 years ago, I was convinced that rice had to be cooked in a rice cooker. When I began living alone in an apartment, a tiny rice cooker was the first thing I bought out of necessity. But, when it broke, and I tried cooking rice in a saucepan, it turned out to be a lot easier than I thought it would be. And it was a lot tastier than the rice I cooked before in that cheap rice cooker. The single-function contraption seemed a waste of space in my small apartment, so I never looked back.

It is perfectly normal for there not to be a rice cooker in a kitchen in the United States, so Americans making Japanese food for the first time are not afraid to cook the rice in a saucepan. Even kids can do it if they follow directions.

When I was teaching the kids in my neighborhood how to cook, I once got an emergency call from one of them. This kid tried cooking 8 cups of rice at one time in a big saucepan. I told the child that I had already explained the maximum you can cook at one time is 3 cups. Apparently it was big party and the child got a bit

てみると、鍋の下のほうはなんとか炊けているものの、上のほうは生米状態。このときは半生の米を5回くらいに分けてボウルに移し、水を加えて電子レンジにかけました。おいしく炊けたごはんとはいえないまでも、食べられるごはんになります。その時のメニューは、マーボー豆腐丼（アメリカ人に好評のメニューの1つ）だったので、ごはんの出来はあまり気にならなかったと思います。

ごはんの保存はお櫃(ひつ)と冷凍が最高

　私は、厚手のステンレスの鍋で炊いたごはんを、お櫃にうつして食卓に出すようにしています。お櫃も単機能で場所をとるし、日本でも今どきどこにでも売っているわけではないので、万人におすすめできるものではありませんが、お櫃にうつしたごはんは余計な水分がとんで、ひときわおいしくなります。また、お櫃の中で冷めたごはんは、炊飯器の中で冷たくなったものとはまったく違う、それなりのおいしさがあります。食事中にテーブルに出しておくにも、木製のお櫃は炊飯器よりずっと風情があり、器として外国人にも好評です。

　余ったごはんは冷凍します。ごはんを1膳(ぜん)分ずつ冷凍

overzealous. I went over to check it out and found that the rice towards the bottom was fine but towards the top it was undercooked. We separated the undercooked rice into about 5 bowls, added some water, and microwaved each bowl. It certainly was not what you would call tasty rice, but it was acceptable. It was destined to go into a bowl and be smothered in mapo tofu (usually a hit with Americans), so the condition of the rice was not essential.

Preserving cooked rice—putting it in an *ohitsu*, a wooden container meant for cooked rice, or the freezer, is best

When I finish cooking my rice in a thick-bottomed stainless steel saucepan, I transfer it to an *ohitsu* and bring it to the dining table. Like a rice cooker, an *ohitsu* has only one function and takes up a bit of space. They are not even sold everywhere in Japan these days, so I do not recommend them for everyone. However, the excess moisture in the cooked rice dissipates after it has been transferred to an *ohitsu* and the rice tastes remarkably better. Also, rice that has been allowed to cool in an *ohitsu* is completely different from rice that has gotten cold in the cooker; it has a taste all its own. The wooden *ohitsu* is also a lovely decoration for the table compared to a rice cooker. Foreigners love them.

Leftover rice should be frozen. Everyone in Japan

するのは日本なら誰でもやっていることですが、電子レンジにかけるだけで炊きたてのようにおいしいごはんが食べられることに、アメリカ人はたいがい「目から鱗」という反応をします。「ごはんを粗末にしてはいけない」という感覚が薄いので、余ったら捨ててしまうアメリカ人も多いのです。とっておくにしても、冷蔵庫に入れてしまってはまずくなり、結局捨てることになりかねません。ですから、ごはんの炊き方を教えたときには必ず冷凍保存方法まで教えることにしています。

ごはんを冷凍するときは、まだ温かいうちにラップに包むことがポイントです。解凍が均等にできるように平たくします。丸く平らにするより、四角くしたほうが保存するのに収まりがいいでしょう。ラップで包んだごはんはさらに冷凍用保存袋にいれて冷凍します。解凍時間は、電子レンジにもよりますが、1膳分で「強」1分20秒から2分くらい。熱いごはんをお茶碗に移したら、すぐに軽くほぐしてこもった蒸気を抜くのがおいしく食べるコツです。

おにぎり：単純だけど難しい力加減

ごはんが炊けたら、次はおにぎりです。おにぎりなん

knows that it should be frozen in single bowlful portions, but when that bowlful of rice is heated up in a microwave oven and savored for the first time, for most Americans it is a moment of enlightenment—the rice tastes just as if it had been freshly cooked. The idea that "not a grain of rice should be wasted" is not prevalent in the United States, so many Americans throw away their leftover rice. If they do save it, they put it in the refrigerator, where it loses its flavor and ultimately has to be thrown out. So, when I teach Americans how to cook rice, I always teach them how to freeze it.

When freezing rice, it is important to wrap it in plastic while it is still warm. Flatten the rice so it defrosts evenly. It is probably wise to make square or rectangular patties out of them as they will fit in the freezer better. After wrapping them in plastic, put them in freezer-proof bags before they go into the freezer. Defrosting times depend on the microwave oven, but generally one bowlful defrosts in about 1 minute 20 seconds to 2 minutes on "high." Transfer the hot rice to a rice bowl and immediately break it up a bit to allow trapped steam to escape—another trick for great tasting rice.

Onigiri—they are simple, but applying just the right pressure is not easy

Now that the rice is cooked, let's make *onigiri*. You may

てわざわざ教えるほどのものか、と思うかもしれませんが、おにぎりを食べたことのない外国人には、ほどよい力で三角や俵型にまとめるというのは意外に難しいものなのです。

アメリカの主婦数人に初めておにぎりのつくりかたを教えたときのことです。まず、私が握って、三角に結ぶ指の形を解説してから、生徒さんたちにつくってもらったところ、できたおにぎりはくっきりと手形のついた平たい塊になっていました。三角にすることができないとか、いびつになるといったことは予想していましたが、まさかごはんで指の型をとったようなものになるとは想像もしていなかったので、びっくり。

初心者なのでごはんが手につかないようにと、ラップを使って握ってもらったのですが、これもかえって災いして、三角形を意識するあまり、力任せに握ってしまったようなのです。子供に教える場合には、最初から普通に握ってもらうことはあきらめて、ラップで茶巾しぼりのようにして丸いおにぎりにしますが、大人だから大丈夫だと思ったのが間違いのもと。日本人が最初からそこそこのおにぎりがつくれるのは、子供のころからおにぎりの食感を知っていて、つくるところを見て育っているからなのだとつくづく思いました。

具が中心になるように握るのはさらに難しいので、まずは具なしおにぎりから始めます。海苔は好みで巻くようにします。

think *onigiri* are so simple that there is no need to teach how to make them, but for foreigners who have never eaten one, using just the right amount of pressure to form them into triangles, circles, and other such shapes can be quite an ordeal.

I remember the first time I tried to teach a group of American housewives how to make *onigiri*. First I shaped one myself, explaining how to make a triangular shape with your fingers. Then I had them try. The results were astonishing—flattish lumps of rice with the shape of their hands clearly imprinted on them. That they may not turn out to be perfect triangles, perhaps somewhat deformed, I was expecting, but I never imagined that I would see the outline of their fingers pressed into them.

Since they were beginners, I let these students use plastic wrap to keep the rice from sticking to their hands—that was inviting disaster. They were overly concerned about the triangular shape and squeezed the *onigiri* with all their might. I had already given up the idea of teaching kids how to make *onigiri* the normal way, so I taught them to make circular ones using plastic wrap, twisting and squeezing with it, but assuming that to be unnecessary with adults was a big mistake. The experience reinforced my belief that Japanese can, for the most part, make *onigiri* from their first try because they have a strong sense of the texture from childhood and grew up watching people making them.

Since it is even more difficult to shape an *onigiri* with a filling in it, we will start with plain *onigiri*. You can wrap them in sheets of *nori* (seaweed) if you like.

茶巾しぼりおにぎり

1. お茶碗など小さいボウルにごはんを入れる。
2. 適当な大きさに切ったラップを広げ、中心にボウルのごはんをあける。
3. ラップの4角をしっかり持ってねじり、茶巾しぼりの要領でごはんを丸くまとめる。
4. まとまったごはんを手の平で握って、三角や俵型など好みの形に整える。
5. 好みで塩やごまをふる。

具を入れる場合

1. 小さいボウルに入れたごはんの真ん中にスプーンで穴をあける。
2. 好みの具（焼いた塩ざけ、梅干など）をくぼみに入れ、その上にひと口分くらいのごはんをかぶせる。
3. 普通のおにぎりと同様に握る。

ごはんもののバリエーション

　白いごはんをマスターしたら、次はごはんのバリエーションです。まぜごはんは、それだけでもお弁当になるし、持ち寄りのパーティーでも喜ばれて、何かと便利なものです。基本を覚えたら好きな素材でいろいろ応用す

Chakin-shibori *onigiri*
(literally *onigiri* squeezed by twisting with a tea cloth, but here we use plastic wrap)

1. Put rice in a rice bowl or other small serving bowl.
2. Lay out a piece of plastic wrap of suitable size; empty the rice out in the center.
3. Lift and firmly hold the 4 corners of the plastic wrap up and twist; continue twisting and squeezing until the rice forms a ball.
4. Shape with the palms of your hands into triangles, ovals, etc.
5. Sprinkle with salt and/or sesame seeds to taste.

Onigiri with fillings

1. Use a spoon to make a hole in the rice in the serving bowl.
2. Place desired filling (grilled salmon, dried plum, etc.) in the hole; cover with a bite-sized lump of rice.
3. Shape as you would plain *onigiri*.

Rice variations

Once you have mastered cooking white rice, you can carry on with some rice variations. *Maze-gohan* (literally "mixed rice") is fine for a boxed lunch on its own, and it is always wonderful to bring to parties. In

ることもできます。

豆ごはん

　ごはんものの中でもアメリカ人に特に人気が高いのは豆ごはん。冷凍グリーンピースだけで手軽にできる上、色合いもきれいなのがうれしいところ。もともと長粒米を使うライス・アンド・ピーズという料理があるので、誰にでも親しみやすい味です。グリーンピースはもちろん生のものを使ってもかまいません。

米	2カップ
水	2〜2¼カップ
酒	大さじ1（好みで）
塩	小さじ⅔
冷凍グリーンピース	⅔カップ

1. 鍋に米と水を入れ、米をこすり合わせるようにしてとぐ。何度も水をかえて水が透き通ってくるまで洗い流す。
2. 水を加え、20分以上そのまま置く（水の計量は正確にし、水が米に均一にかぶるように注意する）。
3. 酒と塩を入れ、よくまぜる。
4. グリーンピースを上に均等にのせる。
5. 蓋をして、弱めの中火で炊く（約15分）。火にかけたあとは、途中でまぜたり、蓋を開けたりしないこと。途中で吹きこぼれそうになったら火を弱める。水がすっかり吸収されたら火を止めて、そのまま10

short, it is very convenient. Once you have learned the basics, you can substitute a wide variety of your favorite ingredients.

Mame-gohan (rice with green peas)

Rice with green peas is a real favorite with Americans. It can be made easily using only frozen green peas. Its colors are also pleasing to the eye. They are already familiar with "rice and peas," which is made using long-grain rice, so anyone can appreciate the taste. Fresh peas, of course, can also be used.

2 cups rice
2 to 2¼ cups water
1 tablespoon sake (or to taste)
⅔ teaspoon salt
⅔ cup frozen green peas

1. Place rice in saucepan. Wash and drain repeatedly until water is clear; drain completely.
2. Add water and let sit for at least 20 minutes (measure water carefully and make sure it evenly the covers rice).
3. Add sake and salt; mix well.
4. Distribute green peas evenly on top.
5. Cover and cook at medium-low (about 15 minutes). After heating, do not stir or remove cover. If it looks like it will spill over, lower the heat. When the water is fully absorbed, turn off the heat; let stand,

分程度蒸らす（蓋はしたまま）。豆をつぶさないように軽くまぜる。

きのこごはん

まぜごはんは具から水分が出るので、水加減をうまく調節しないとやわらかくなりすぎてしまいます。最初に具を調理して、その煮汁と水を一緒に計量すれば失敗なくつくれます。

米 ………… 2カップ
きのこ（好みのもの）……… 1パック（きざんで2カップ程度）
煮汁 ……… (醤油大さじ2、酒大さじ1、水½カップ)
水 ………… 適宜

1. きのこ（シイタケ、えのきだけ、エリンギ、まいたけ、しめじなど）は食べやすい大きさにきざんでおく。
2. 煮汁の材料で、きざんだきのこを火が通るまで煮る（5分程度）。
3. 煮汁を切って、きのこはとっておく。
4. 煮汁に水を加えて2〜2¼カップにし、米に加え、白米と同様に炊く。
5. 炊き上がったら、きのこをごはんの上に入れ、すぐに蓋をして、そのまま10分程度蒸らす。さっくりと空気を入れるようにまぜる。

covered, 10 minutes. Mix gently to avoid crushing the peas.

Rice with mushrooms

The rice will absorb water from other ingredients in *maze-gohan*, so if you are not careful about adjusting the amount of water, you will end up with rice that is too soft. If you cook the other items first, retaining the cooking liquid, and count the liquid as a part of the water used for cooking the rice, you will avoid failure every time.

2 cups rice
2 cups chopped mushrooms (any type you like)
Cooking liquid: 2 tablespoons soy sauce,
 1 tablespoon sake, ½ cup water
Water as needed

1. Cut up mushrooms (*shiitake, enoki, eringi, maitake, shimeji*, etc.) into bite-sized pieces.
2. Boil mushrooms in cooking liquid until cooked through (about 5 minutes).
3. Turn off heat; remove mushrooms.
4. Add enough water to cooking liquid to obtain 2 to 2¼ cups. Add rice; cook as you would plain white rice.
5. When rice is cooked, distribute mushrooms on top; cover immediately and let steam 10 minutes. Mix well, aerating the rice.

＊ベジタリアンにもOK

どういうわけか、アメリカには大人にも子供にもベジタリアンが結構います。宗教的なベジタリアンも中にはいますが、ほとんどは健康志向のベジタリアンです。ティーンエイジャーや子供の場合、動物愛護の精神から動物を食べない、というケースが多いようです（ただの偏食という場合もありますが）。

大勢のパーティーには、ベジタリアンでも食べられる料理が1品くらいはあったほうが安心です。ごはんものには肉やシーフードを使ったまぜごはんより、野菜のみの精進のほうが登場機会が圧倒的に多くなります。特に、わからないくらい細かくきざんだ肉やシーフードが入っているタイプの料理はベジタリアンには危険だし、肉好き、魚好きにも今ひとつ受けません。

玄米

白米に対するこだわりが少ない分、アメリカ人には玄米ファンが多くいます。自然食のレストランでなく、ごく普通の日本料理店や中華料理店でも、ごはんは白米か玄米のいずれかを選べるようになっています。玄米は白米より、炊くのにかなり時間がかかりますが、手間は同じです。

玄米の場合、とぐ必要はありませんが、洗うときに水に浮かびやすいのでザルを使って水を切ります。水は白米より多く必要で、炊く時間も長くかかります。途中で蓋をあけて様子を見てもかまいません。

* Okay for vegetarians
  For whatever reason, there are quite a few vegetarians in the United States, both children and adults. There are some who are vegetarians for religious reasons, but the majority of them are vegetarians for their health. Teenagers and children seem to become vegetarians out of concern for animal rights (but some are just fussy about their food).
  When holding a big party, it is always wise to have at least one vegetarian dish. This is an opportunity just waiting for you to try making maze-gohan using vegetables only, instead of meat and seafood. Vegetarians are particularly wary of food with meat or seafood minced up so finely it can hardly be detected, and it does not appeal to meat and seafood lovers, either.

Brown rice

Americans may not be heavily "into" their white rice, but many of them certainly are great fans of brown rice. You are offered a choice of white or brown rice not only at natural food restaurants, but at ordinary Japanese and Chinese restaurants, as well. It takes a fair bit longer to cook brown rice than it does white rice, but the tasks involved are the same.

You do not need to rub the grains together when you wash brown rice, but it tends to float easily, so use a strainer to drain the water. As mentioned, it takes more time to cook brown rice, but it also requires more water. You can, however, remove the cover from time to time to see how it is doing.

まずごはんを炊こう

玄米………2カップ
水…………2.5カップ
昆布………3センチ角くらい（なくても可）

1. 玄米を鍋に入れてざっと洗い、ザルにあげる。
2. 鍋に玄米、水、昆布を入れ、そのまま置いて水を吸わせる（2時間以上、できればひと晩）。
3. 弱めの中火にかけ、煮立ってきたら弱火にし、水分がなくなって上のほうの玄米がやわらかくなるまで炊く（30分〜50分）。火加減や給水時間によって炊く時間がかなり違ってくるため、ときどき蓋をあけて様子を見る。表面に水分がなくなっていても、下に水分がたまっていて、表面の玄米が炊けていない場合もあるので注意。
4. 火を止めて、そのまま10分程度蒸らす。昆布をとり除き、上下を返しながら空気を入れるようにまぜる。

2 cups brown rice
2½ cups water
3 cm square piece *konbu* (kelp, optional)

1. Put rice in saucepan and wash quickly; drain in a strainer.
2. Return rice to saucepan; add water and *konbu*. Leave to absorb water for at least 2 hours, preferably overnight.
3. Heat at medium-low until boiling; turn to low. Cook until water is gone and the rice on top is soft, about 30 to 50 minutes. Since the cooking time depends on the heat and the time it takes to absorb water, remove the lid and check the progress from time to time. There are times when the water is gone from the surface but remains below, and the rice on the top may still not have cooked through.
4. Turn off the heat and let steam 10 minutes. Remove *konbu*; mix well, turning over and aerating the rice.

2

お寿司
Sushi

誤解の多い日本料理の代表選手

　今や日本食といえば「スシ」というほど、お寿司は海外で人気の日本料理です。その人気はすき焼きや天ぷらをはるかにしのいでいます。アメリカでは、日本料理店ばかりか、中華料理店や韓国料理店のメニューにも寿司が載り、ごく普通のスーパーのデリコーナーでも寿司セットはもはや定番。ですから、アメリカ人に日本料理を教える場合も、ごはんの炊き方をマスターしたら、次は寿司です。

　これだけ大人気の寿司ですが、寿司といえば江戸前のにぎり寿司しか知られていないので、「寿司イコール生魚」という思い込みも多く、ほとんどのアメリカ人が日本語の「スシ」と「サシミ」を混同して理解しています。
　日本語で「スシ」というのは酢飯を用いた料理一般のことで、本来は発酵による保存食（なれ寿司）の意味でしたが、そのことを知る外国人はほとんどいないでしょう。寿司はベジタリアン料理としてもつくれるし、巻き物やにぎり寿司ばかりが寿司ではない、と言うと、皆一様に意外そうな顔をします。レストランで出てくるようなにぎり寿司は家庭でつくるものではなく、あれは専門店だけで食べるものだ、と言うと、さらに意外そうな表情になります。

　でも、巻いたり握ったりする技術がなくても、魚が苦

The often-misunderstood Japanese champion

Going out to eat Japanese means going out to eat sushi. It is that popular overseas. Its popularity far exceeds that of sukiyaki or tempura. In the United States you will find sushi on the menu in many Chinese and Korean restaurants, not to mention probably all Japanese restaurants, and it is a standard item in the deli section of an ordinary supermarket. Therefore, when teaching Americans how to prepare Japanese food, sushi obviously has to follow the mastering of cooking rice.

Most Americans equate sushi with raw fish, getting sushi mixed up at times with sashimi, because they are only familiar with *Edomae nigiri-zushi* (hand-molded sushi using raw fish).

The Japanese word "sushi" is a general one referring to food that uses sushi rice (*sumeshi*). It originated with a preserved food known as *nare-zushi*, fermented fish and rice, but there are very few Americans who know this. When I tell them that sushi can easily suit the vegetarians' palate, and it is not limited to just sushi rolls and hand-molded sushi, everyone looks surprised. This expression becomes more exaggerated when I tell them that Japanese do not actually make at home the sushi they are so used to being served in restaurants—we go to specialty shops for that!

But, even if you lack rolling and shaping skills, or

手でも寿司はつくれるということは日本料理初心者にとってはうれしい驚きです。まずは、技術がなくても日本料理店で食べるスシと近いものが味わえる手巻き寿司から始めましょう。

酢飯のつくり方：おいしい酢飯が寿司の要

　寿司の基本は酢飯です。炊き方は、ほとんど普通のごはんと変わりませんが、いくつかコツがあります。まず、水加減を控えめにすること。炊き上がってからすし酢をかけるので、その分堅めに炊き上げないと、ベチャッとした酢飯になってしまいます。次に、ごはんが炊き上がったら、すぐにすし酢をまぜて、手早く冷ますこと。ごはんとすし酢をまぜるには大きめのボウルを使い、米粒をつぶさないようにサックリとまぜます。小さいボウルで無理をしてまぜるとごはんがつぶれてしまうので、ボウルは必ず大きめの、できるだけ平たい形のものを用いてください。木製のサラダボウルがおすすめです。もちろん日本の飯台（はんだい）があればそれが一番です。見た目がいいばかりでなく、お櫃（ひつ）と同様に水分をほどよく吸って、適度な通気性と保温性が酢飯をぐんとおいしくします。飯台はまぜごはんなどのお櫃代わりにも使えますし、私は日本食でのおもてなしには必需品だと思っています。

just dislike fish, you can still make sushi. That is a pleasant surprise for beginners. Let's begin with hand-rolled sushi—it is easy to make and tastes a lot like what you get in Japanese restaurants.

How to make sushi rice —it is essential for good sushi

Sushi rice is the very foundation for sushi. The way to cook it is almost identical to the way you cook ordinary rice, but there are a couple of tricks involved. The first trick is to keep the amount of water on the low side. Since you will be adding sushi vinegar after the rice is cooked, it has to be just a little bit on the firm side; otherwise, it will become mushy. The next trick is to mix in the sushi vinegar right after the rice is finished cooking and cool it quickly. You need to use a large bowl to mix the sushi vinegar into the rice. Mix in a slicing manner being, careful not to crush the rice grains. Use a wide, somewhat flat bowl if you can—remember, if you try to do this in a small bowl, you will crush the rice grains. A wooden salad bowl works well. Of course, a Japanese sushi rice tub is made for the job, so it is perfect. It not only looks good, but like an *ohitsu*, it removes excess moisture, allows just enough air passage, and keeps the rice warm. A Japanese sushi rice tub can also second as an *ohitsu* to keep *maze-gohan* and other rice dishes tasting good. I find this item an essential

お米は白米のほか、胚芽米でもつくれます。アメリカでは健康志向に合わせた玄米の巻き寿司も見かけますが、お味のほうは今ひとつ。玄米は堅く炊いたのではすし酢を吸ってくれないし、うまく巻いたり握ったりできません。ですから、お米が割れるほどやわらかく炊くことになり、ベタベタしてしまうのです。また、お料理によってはかえっておいしく感じられる玄米ならではの風味もお寿司には今ひとつ合いません。

酢飯

米 …………2カップ
水 …………2カップ（酒を使う場合はここから大さじ2杯分の水を減らす）
酒 …………大さじ2（好みで）
昆布………3センチ角1枚（好みで）
すし酢……大さじ5 （米酢大さじ4、砂糖大さじ1、塩小さじ1.5を溶けるまでまぜます）

*すし酢は市販のすし酢を使ってもかまいません。すし酢は常備しておくと、酢飯のほかにも酢の物やサラダドレッシングなどにも使えて便利です。

1. ふつうにごはんを炊くのと同様に米をとぐ。
2. 水を加え20分以上置く。
3. 酒を加えてよくまぜてから、昆布を入れる。

"performer" when serving Japanese dishes.

In addition to white rice, sushi rice can be made with *haiga* rice. In the United States, hot on the heels of the health food boom, even sushi made from brown rice can be found, but it does not taste very good. If the brown rice is cooked on the firm side, it will not absorb the vinegar, nor will it roll well or shape easily in your hands. You really have to cook it until it is so soft the grains break apart, but then it gets gummy. While the taste and texture of brown rice improves some dishes, the very same qualities make it less suitable for sushi.

Sushi rice

2 cups rice
2 cups water (if adding sake, reduce water by 2 tablespoons)
2 tablespoons sake (optional)
3-cm square piece of *konbu* (optional)
5 tablespoons sushi vinegar: 4 tablespoons rice vinegar, 1 tablespoon sugar, 1½ teaspoons salt, stirred in until dissolved
*You can use store-bought sushi vinegar. It is handy to have around the kitchen for making *su-no-mono* (vinegared vegetables), salad dressings, and a variety of other dishes.

1. Place rice in saucepan; wash and drain several times.
2. Add water; let soak for at least 20 minutes.
3. Add sake; mix well. Add *konbu*.

4 弱めの中火にかけ、沸騰してきたら弱火にして水分がなくなるまで炊く（約15分）。
5 火からおろし、そのまま蓋をとらずに10分蒸らす。
6 飯台または大きめのボウルにごはんをあけ、すし酢をまわしかけて、しゃもじでサックリと切るようにまぜ合わせる。まぜながら時々うちわであおぐと余分な水気がとんでうまく冷める。酢がごはんにまざって吸収され、人肌くらいに冷めたらぬらしてしぼった布巾またはペーパータオルをかけて乾燥しないようにしておく。

*すし酢をまぜるときにうちわであおいでくれる人が別にいると楽。子供のお手伝いに格好の仕事。

① 飯台または、大きめのボウルに ごはんをあける

② すし酢をまわしかけ、ザックリと切るようにまぜ合わせる

時々、うちわであおぎ、余分な水気をとばす

③ 人肌ぐらいに冷めたら ぬらしてしぼった布巾か ペーパータオルをかけておく

4. Cover and heat on medium-low. When the water reaches a boil, reduce heat to low; cook until water is fully absorbed (about 15 minutes).
5. Remove from heat; let steam, covered, 10 minutes.
6. Empty rice into sushi tub or big bowl; pour sushi vinegar over rice. Using a rice paddle, mix rice in slicing motions. While mixing, occasionally fan the rice; doing so will cool the rice faster and remove excess moisture. When the rice has absorbed the vinegar and cooled to about body temperature, cover with a damp cloth or paper towels to keep it from drying out.

* It is nice to have somebody do the fanning while you mix the sushi rice; a good job for any kids that are around.

---

1. Empty rice into a sushi tub or big bowl.
2. Using a rice paddle, mix rice in slicing motions. While mixing, occasionally fan the rice to remove excess moisture.
3. When the rice has cooled to about body temperature, cover with a damp, wrung out cloth or paper towel.

簡単豪華な手巻き寿司

　現在の日本の家庭では、ホームメイドのお寿司といえば、ちらし寿司や巻き寿司より手巻き寿司のほうがポピュラーなのではないでしょうか。材料を切るだけで手軽にできて、量の調節もしやすく、具によって豪華にもカジュアルにもなります。ただ、海外の場合には新鮮な刺身の入手が困難です。そこで、まず試してみたいのがカリフォルニアロールの手巻き。アメリカ生まれのカリフォルニアロールはカニときゅうりとアボカドを巻いたもの。カニはカニかまぼこでかまいません。上等のカニをたっぷり使えるなら話は別ですが、カリフォルニアロールの場合には、下手に本物のカニを使うよりカニかまぼこのほうが扱いやすく、おいしくできます。

カリフォルニアロールの手巻き

酢飯……………お茶碗4杯分
海苔(のり)……………4〜5枚（1枚を4つの正方形に切るとちょうどよい大きさになる）
きゅうり…………1〜2本
カニかまぼこ……1パック
アボカド…………1個
わさび、醤油(しょうゆ)

Simple yet deluxe hand-rolled sushi

I think it is safe to say that hand-rolled sushi is a more popular homemade sushi these days in Japan than *chirashi-zushi* (sushi rice with ingredients simply "scattered" on top) and sushi rolls. All you have to do is cut up the ingredients. It is easy to adjust the volume of the ingredients, and depending on your selection, they can be as deluxe or as casual as you would like. However, it is difficult to get fresh sashimi overseas, so, let's begin with hand-rolled California rolls. Born in the United States, California rolls use crab meat, cucumber, and avocado. You can substitute crab sticks if you would like. It is another matter if you are going to use the highest grade of crab meat, but, in general, with California rolls, it is easier and probably less risky to use crab sticks than ordinary crab meat.

Hand-rolled california rolls

4 bowls of sushi rice
4 to 5 sheets of *nori* (1 sheet cut into 4 squares is just the right size)
1 or 2 cucumbers
1 package crab sticks
1 avocado
Wasabi and soy sauce

1. 海苔はあらかじめ1枚を4つの正方形に切っておく。封が切り立てのパリッとした海苔なら、4つ折りにして手で割くだけできれいに4等分できる。うまく割けない場合にはハサミを使って切る。
2. きゅうりは長さ10センチくらいに切ってから、縦に棒状に切る（日本のきゅうりの場合、4等分か6等分が適当）。アメリカの太いきゅうりを使う場合には、皮をむいて種を除いてから8等分に。または、長さ10センチくらいに切って、かつらむきしてから千切りにする。
3. アボカドは2つに割ってから種を除き、皮をむいて、縦に6等分する。

＊手巻きの巻き方
手の平に海苔を置き、適量の酢飯をのせてスプーンで軽く広げ、その上に具を置いて巻く。わさびは好みで具と一緒に巻いても、醤油に溶いてつけてもかまわない。酢飯の量を控えめにするのがうまく巻くコツ。

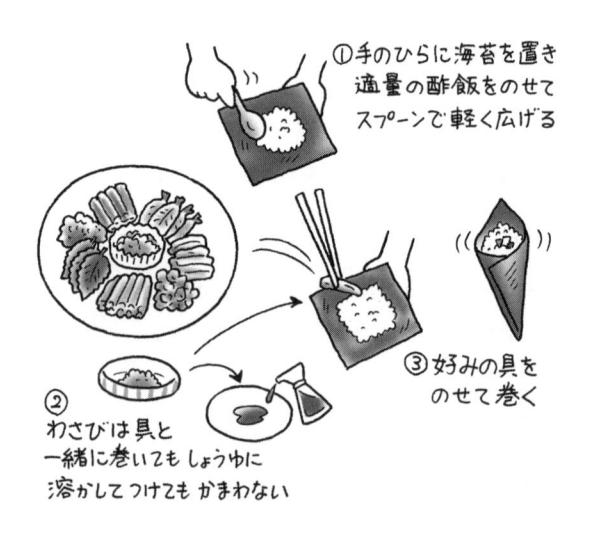

①手のひらに海苔を置き適量の酢飯をのせてスプーンで軽く広げる

②わさびは具と一緒に巻いてもしょうゆに溶かしてつけてもかまわない

③好みの具をのせて巻く

1. Cut each sheet of *nori* into 4 squares. If the pouch has been freshly opened, you can easily fold the sheets in 4 and tear them into 4 equal pieces. If that does not work you can use scissors instead.
2. Cut cucumber into 10-cm lengths, then cut lengthwise to make strips (4 to 6 strips if using a Japanese cucumber). Cucumbers in the United States are thicker; they should have their skin and seeds removed. Divide them into 8 equal strips. Alternatively, you can cut them in 10-cm lengths and use the *katsura-muki* technique to peel them; after peeling, julienne.
3. Divide avocado in two; remove seed, peel off skin, and cut lengthwise into 6 equal strips.

* Making hand-rolled sushi
Place the *nori* in the palm of your hand. Put some sushi rice on it and spread gently with a spoon. Place the fillings on top and roll. You can add wasabi along with the fillings, or stir it into soy sauce, dipping the hand rolls in the mixture as you eat. The trick to making hand rolls is not overdoing it with the sushi rice.

---

1. Place the *nori* in the palm of your hand; put some sushi rice on it and spread gently with a spoon.
2. Add wasabi along with the fillings or dip in a soy sauce/wasabi mix while eating.
3. Place fillings on top and roll.

*かつらむき

皮をむく要領で、きゅうりを回しながらできるだけ薄くむいていく。種が出てきたところで切り、種の部分（芯の部分）は捨てる。

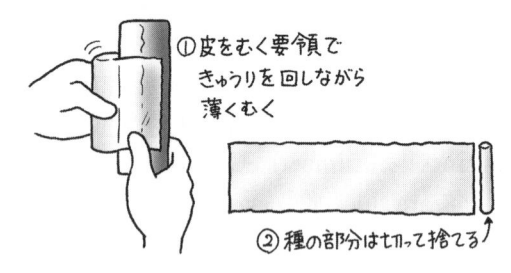

①皮をむく要領で
きゅうりを回しながら
薄くむく

②種の部分は切って捨てる

*アボカドの種のとり方と切り方

アボカドは皮のついたまま、縦2つになるように種の周りを切る。実の両側を持ってねじると、種がどちらか片側について2つに割れるので、種のついているほうを持ち、種にナイフを刺してねじると簡単に取れる（ナイフの先端ではなく、歯をあてて固定するようにします）。

① 皮つきのまま
縦2つになるよう
種の周りを切る

② 実の両側を
持ってねじる

③ 種がどちらか片側に
ついて 2つに割れる

* *Katsura-muki* technique

With a sharp knife, turn the cucumber as you peel as thinly as possible, as if you were removing the skin. Stop when you reach any seeds and discard the core.

---

1. Peel thinly, turning the cucumber, as if removing the skin.
2. Cut off when seeds are reached and discard core.

* Cutting and removing the seed from an avocado

Without removing the skin, cut the avocado in two, lengthwise, around the seed. Grasp both sides and twist in two; the seed will remain on one side or the other. It can then be removed easily with a knife (do not use the tip of the knife; use the heel, as shown in the illustration).

④ 種がついているほうを持ち
種にナイフを刺してねじる

簡単に取れる

---

1. With the skin on, cut the avocado in two, lengthwise, around the seed.
2. Grasp both sides and twist.
3. The avocado will come apart with the seed on one or the other side.
4. Holding the side with the seed, cut into the seed with a knife and twist. The seed will come out easily.

＊海苔の保存法
海苔は湿気が大敵。開封したら、すべて4等分した上で保存用ビニール袋に入れて冷凍しておくと、しけることなく便利に使える。

手巻きの具

何でも巻けるのが手巻き寿司のいいところ。定番からちょっと変わったものまで、具のアイデアをご紹介します。手巻きの具として合わないもののほうが珍しいくらいなので、このほかにもいろいろお試しください。

魚

寿司といえば、やはり刺身。新鮮な刺身ならそのまま切るだけで十分ですが、ちょっと手を加えると味に変化をもたせることができます。また、前日にあらかじめ準備できるので、当日に買い物に行けない場合に助かります。火を通すわけではないので、魚は必ず刺身用のものを用いてください。

そのほか、おなじみのツナ缶や天ぷらがあれば、生魚が苦手な人にも安心です。

* Preserving *nori*

  Moisture is its biggest enemy, so once a package of *nori* is opened, divide all the sheets into 4 equal smaller sheets and freeze in a plastic freezer bag. This way they are easy to use and will not get stale.

Other ingredients that can be used as fillings for hand-rolled sushi

The great thing about hand rolls is that anything can be used as a filling. Here are some ideas, from standard to somewhat unusual fillings. It is very uncommon to find something that does not work well in a hand roll, so enjoy coming up with your own ideas.

Fish

Sashimi is integral to sushi. All you have to do is slice fresh sashimi, but by taking some extra steps you can create something special. In addition, these steps can be taken the day before serving, so they come in handy when you cannot go shopping on the day of the meal. Remember that none of these involve cooking the fish, so make sure you use only "sashimi quality."

In addition to these, canned tuna, tempura, and other such ingredients can be used; this is reassuring to those who do not like raw fish.

昆布締め

刺身をサクのまま、酒でしめらせた昆布にはさんでラップに包み、冷蔵庫にひと晩置きます。昆布にはさむときには刺身全体が昆布にぴったり密着するようにすること。ヒラメなどの白身の魚やサケが合います。

ヅケ

マグロを醤油漬けにしたヅケは伝統的な江戸前寿司のネタ。手巻きの具にもぴったりです。

密閉容器に醤油大さじ2、酒大さじ1、みりん大さじ1をまぜ、マグロのサク1つをペーパータオルにくるんで漬け汁が全体にまわるようにしてから密閉し、1時間からひと晩おきます。ペーパータオルにくるむことで少ない漬け汁でもマグロ全体に味がまわります。

ごま漬け

刺身用の魚を食べやすい大きさに切ってから漬け込みます。サク1つ分程度の刺身に対し、つけ汁は醤油、みりん、すりごまを各大さじ1。切った刺身とともに密閉容器に入れてよくまぜ、1時間からひと晩おきます。好みであさつきの小口切りやしその葉の千切りをまぜます。お茶漬けの具としてもおすすめです。

Konbu-jime (fish marinated with kelp)

Wrap whole pieces (blocks) of sashimi-quality fish in *konbu* which has been soaked in sake; wrap in plastic and place in the refrigerator overnight. Ensure that every bit of the fish is in contact with the *konbu*. White-fleshed fish varieties such as flounder work well; salmon is also tasty.

Zuke (marinating)

Tuna marinated in soy sauce is a tradition going back to *Edomae* sushi. It is great in hand-rolled sushi, as well.

Combine 2 tablespoons soy sauce, 1 tablespoon sake, and 1 tablespoon *mirin* in an air-tight container. Wrap whole pieces (blocks) of tuna in paper towels and soak thoroughly in the liquid; close cover and refrigerate for 1 hour to overnight. The use of paper towels enables the marinating of a large quantity of tuna with a relatively small amount of liquid.

Goma-zuke (marinating in ground sesame seed)

Cut sashimi-quality fish into bite-size portions. One whole piece of sashimi (one block) requires about 1 tablespoon each of soy sauce, *mirin*, and ground sesame seed. Mix well with the sliced sashimi in an air-tight container; cover and marinate in the refrigerator for 1 hour to overnight. Mix in chopped chives, julienned *shiso*, or other aromatics to taste. This is great as a topping for *ochazuke* (usually leftover rice heated up by pouring green tea over it, with various toppings). Give it a try.

スパイシーツナ

アメリカの寿司の定番メニュー。生のねぎとろでもツナ缶でもできます。いずれの場合も、マヨネーズ、醬油、ラー油で味つけし、あさつきまたは万能ねぎの小口切りをまぜ込みます。調味料は味をみながら好みで加えてください（ツナ1缶に対して、マヨネーズ大さじ2、醬油小さじ1、ラー油小さじ1/2程度が目安）。おにぎりの具にしてもいけます。

天ぷら （詳しいつくり方は210ページ）

エビの天ぷらはアメリカの寿司ネタの定番です。魚は嫌いでもエビだけは食べるという外国人や子供は多くいます。

野菜

きゅうりは定番の具ですが、そのほか、しその葉、あさつき、かいわれ大根、クレソン、みょうがなど香りのある野菜や巻きやすい野菜なら何でもOKです。また、アボカドはカリフォルニアロールだけでなく、たいていの魚に合い、アボカドと野菜だけの手巻きはベジタリアンのお客様に好評です。サニーレタスやサラダ菜など、やわらかい葉物を海苔のかわりにしたサラダ手巻きもおすすめ。外国人には海苔が苦手な人も意外に多いので用意しておくと安心です。

Spicy tuna

This is now a standard item on sushi menus in the United States. You use raw *negitoro* (the fatty, belly part of a tuna, chopped and mixed with scallions) or canned tuna. Whichever you use, it should be flavored with mayonnaise, soy sauce, and hot sesami oil; mix in thin slices of chives or scallions. Taste as you prepare to get the proportions that work best for you (as a guideline, for one can of tuna, use about 2 tablespoons mayonnaise, 1 teaspoon soy sauce, and ½ teaspoon hot sesami oil). This makes a great filling for *onigiri*, too.

Tempura (see page 211 for directions)

Shrimp tempura is also a standard ingredient on sushi menus in the United States. There are many foreigners and their kids who do not like fish but like shrimp.

Vegetables

Cucumber is a standard filling, but other aromatic and easily rolled vegetables, such as *shiso*, chives, white radish sprouts, watercress, and *myoga* (Japanese ginger) work well, too. Avocados have their role outside of the California roll. They go well with most fish, and alone they are a vegetarian's delight. You could even use sunny lettuce or another soft-leafed variety to replace the *nori* for wrapping; in fact, a surprising number of foreigners do not like *nori*, so it is good to have some of this on hand.

肉

寿司屋で出すお寿司に肉は使いませんが、家庭の手巻きなら肉もありです。子供にも好評です。

照り焼き （詳しいつくり方は202ページ）

鶏肉でも牛肉でも豚肉でもかまいませんが、お寿司は温かい料理ではないので、脂身の多い部分は向きません。テフロン加工のフライパンで焼き、火が通ったところで醤油とみりん同量をまわしかけます。巻きやすく細長く切って、ねぎやしその葉などと一緒にどうぞ。

ローストビーフ

ローストビーフにはねぎやわさび醤油がよく合います。

薬味類

わさび

寿司にはわさびがなくては始まりません。アメリカにはわさび好きが多く、アメリカ人の多いパーティーだと、小ぶりのお茶碗に粉わさびをたっぷり練っておいてもなくなってしまうことがあります。理由はその使い方にもあります。アメリカではレストランでも寿司はすべて「さび抜き」で、各自が別添えのわさびを醤油に溶いて使うのが一般的です。醤油のつぎ方も、つけ醤油というよりはディップソース感覚でなみなみとつぐので、自然にわさびの消費量も多くなるようなのです。

Meat

Sushi restaurants do not use meat, but there is no reason you cannot use meat at home. Kids love it, too.

Teriyaki-style (see page 203 for detailed instructions)
Chicken, beef, pork—they all work well, but sushi is not intended to be served hot, so fatty cuts should be avoided. Cook in a Teflon-coated frying pan; when cooked through, stir in equal amounts of soy sauce and *mirin*. Cut in narrow, easy-to-wrap strips. Try it combined with scallions or *shiso* leaves.

Roast beef
Roast beef goes well with the likes of scallions and a wasabi/soy sauce mix.

Condiments

Wasabi
Wasabi is essential to sushi. Many Americans are very fond of wasabi. For a party with a lot of Americans attending, you can fill a small bowl full of wasabi powder, mix it up, and it will be gone by the end of the party. The reason for this is the way they use it. Sushi at restaurants in the United States is served wasabi-less, so one mixes wasabi into soy sauce at the table. And the amount of soy sauce they pour out is a far cry from the teaspoon or so that Japanese use—it becomes more like a dipping sauce for spring rolls. This, naturally, leads to

しょうが

　しょうがの甘酢漬けはなければいけないというものではありませんが、あると寿司らしい気分になります。

ごま

　白ごまを香ばしく炒ったものは何にでも合います。

寿司屋では食べられないちらし寿司

　私が子供のころ、ホームメイドの寿司といえばちらし寿司に決まっていたようなものでした。寿司屋にも「ちらし」というメニューはありますが、あれは酢飯に刺身をのせたもので、家庭でつくるちらしとは名前は同じでも別物ということを日本人なら子供のころから経験的に知っています。アメリカのスシレストランにも「ちらし」は必ずメニューにありますが、アメリカ人にとって家庭でつくるちらし寿司は、日本人の家庭に招かれない限り食べるチャンスはありません。アメリカ人は、「ちらし」といえば、寿司屋のちらしを思い浮かべます。そのため、家庭のちらしとは寿司屋のものとは別物であるということを説明するところから始めます。

　日本では、地方や家庭の習慣によって、ちらし寿司に

an overconsumption of wasabi.

Ginger

You can get away without having sweet, pickled ginger, but it sort of lends an air of "sushiness" to the atmosphere.

Sesame

Fragrant, toasted, white sesame seeds—these go well with everything.

Chirashi-zushi (literally, "scattered sushi") —not available at sushi restaurants

When I was a kid, *chirashi-zushi* was the only homemade sushi I knew of. There exists "*chirashi*" on menus in sushi shops in Japan, but that is sashimi on top of sushi rice—the same name, but not the same as what is prepared at home, as anyone who grew up in Japan knows. It follows that "*chirashi*" is on sushi menus in the United States, as well, but Americans do not know the difference between it and the home version because they have never had a chance to try it, unless they have been invited to the home of a Japanese family. Americans only know of the *chirashi* served at sushi restaurants. I will begin by explaining the difference between home and restaurant *chirashi-zushi*.

In Japan, depending on the region or a family's

穴子や酢じめの魚やジャコをいれることもありますが、私はちらしはまず精進の寿司として教えています。材料の入手が簡単ということもありますが、寿司は必ずしも魚料理ではなく、野菜だけでもつくれるということを知ってほしいからです。

精進のちらし寿司

　お寿司初心者でもつくりやすいように材料を限定し、できるだけ簡素化したレシピです。具としては、このほかにごぼうや、こんにゃく、高野豆腐などを甘辛く煮て細かく切ったものなどを加えれば、より風味が豊かになります。卵は薄焼きにするのが一般的ですが、つくるにもきざむにも手先の器用さが必要なので、かきまぜるだけでつくれるそぼろ卵にしました。緑も最も手軽な材料として冷凍グリーンピースを使ってありますが、絹さやをゆでてきざんだものなど、ほかの緑の野菜でもかまいません。赤（にんじん）、黄（卵）、緑（グリーンピース）の入った華やかな色合いがちらし寿司の要です。

own traditions, sometimes such ingredients as conger eel, vinegared fish, or dried baby sardine are used, but I adhere to keeping *chirashi-zushi* strictly vegetarian. This is partially because the ingredients are easy to find, but also because I want it to be understood that *chirashi-zushi* does not need to be limited to only fish; vegetables alone are fine for *chirashi-zushi*.

A purist's approach to *chirashi-zushi*

I have intentionally simplified this recipe, limiting the ingredients, so even the sushi beginner can achieve good results. The addition of other ingredients can only add richness to it—these include burdock root, *konnyaku*, and freeze-dried tofu, simmered in sweet/salty liquid and sliced thinly. Eggs are usually cooked very thin and cut into sliver-like strips, but that takes quite a bit of dexterity, so in this recipe we will scramble and mince them. We use frozen green peas for a lovely green color, but slices of snow peas or another green vegetable could also be used. *Chirashi-zushi* has to be colorful, so you need red (carrot), yellow (egg), and green (peas).

〈酢飯〉

米 …………2カップ

水 …………2カップ（酒を使う場合はここから大さじ2杯分の水を減らす）

酒 …………大さじ2（好みで）

昆布…………3センチ角1枚（好みで）

すし酢………大さじ5（米酢大さじ4、砂糖大さじ1、塩小さじ1.5を溶けるまでまぜる）

〈具〉

しいたけ……（干ししいたけ5～6枚、醤油(しょうゆ)大さじ1、砂糖大さじ1）

にんじん……（小1本、塩少々、酒大さじ1）

卵 …………（3個、砂糖大さじ1）

グリーンピース ………（冷凍グリーンピース適量をゆでておく）

1 まず酢飯をつくる（つくり方は66ページ）。

2 しいたけはかぶるくらいの水に浸して、浮いてこないように皿などで重しをし、冷蔵庫にひと晩置いて戻す。しいたけが完全に戻ったら細切りにし、戻し汁に水を足して、それでしいたけを煮る。途中で水が足りなくなったら少しずつ足しながら、常にしいたけに水がかぶるくらいにして30分程度煮る。調味料を加え、水分がほとんどなくなるまでさらに煮る。

3 にんじんは斜めに薄く切ってから細い千切りにし、ひたひたの水に塩少々と酒を加えて水気がなくなるまで煮る（5～10分）。

Sushi rice

2 cups rice

2 cups water (if adding sake, reduce water by 2 tablespoons)

2 tablespoons sake (optional)

3-cm square piece of *konbu* (optional)

5 tablespoons sushi vinegar: 4 tablespoons rice vinegar, 1 tablespoon sugar, 1½ teaspoons salt, stirred in until dissolved

Ingredients

Shiitake mushrooms (5 to 6 dried *shiitake* mushrooms, 1 tablespoon soy sauce, 1 tablespoon sugar)

Carrot (1 small carrot, pinch of salt, 1 tablespoon sake)

Egg (3 eggs, 1 tablespoon sugar)

Green peas (boil green peas as needed)

1. First make the sushi rice (see page 67 for details).
2. Add just enough water to the dried *shiitake* mushrooms to cover them; place a dish on top to keep them from floating and soak in the refrigerator overnight. When the *shiitake* mushrooms are fully rehydrated, slice them into thin strips. Add some more water to the soaking liquid and simmer the *shiitake* mushrooms for about 30 minutes; add water if necessary so that *shiitake* mushrooms are always covered in water. Add seasonings and continue to simmer until most of the liquid is gone.
3. Thinly slice the carrot on the diagonal then julienne. Lightly submerge in water; add salt and sake. Simmer until the liquid disappears, about 5 to 10 minutes.

④ 卵をほぐして砂糖を入れ、さらによくまぜて砂糖を溶かす。テフロン加工の小型の鍋に卵液を入れて弱火にかける。割り箸4本を使って常にかきまぜ続け、できるだけ細かいそぼろ状にする。完全に火が通ったら火からおろし、さらにしばらくかきまぜ続けると、パラリとしたきれいな卵のそぼろになる。

⑤ 酢飯がまだ温かいうちににんじんとしいたけをまぜる。平らな器に盛って（飯台を使って酢飯をつくった場合には飯台をそのまま使う）、そぼろ卵を全体に散らし、その上からゆでたグリーンピースを散らす。

*干ししいたけの戻し方

干ししいたけは時間をかけてじっくり戻したほうがおいしくなり、栄養価も損なわれません。冷蔵庫で24時間以上かけるのが理想です。2〜3日おいても大丈夫なので、思いついたときに水を加えて密閉容器に入れ、冷蔵しておくといつでも使えて便利です（ただし3日以上保存する場合は冷凍します）。私は干ししいたけを開封したら、1袋全部戻してしまいます。やわらかく戻ったら数個ずつラップにくるんで冷凍したり、醤油と砂糖で煮つけてから小分けにして冷凍します。これはとても重宝します。時間がないときには電子レンジで戻す方法（ひたひたの水を加えてラップをかけ数分加熱）もありますが、味は落ちます。まとめて戻したしいたけを冷凍で常備するほうがおすすめです。

4. Beat the eggs; add sugar and beat until dissolved. In a small Teflon-coated frying pan, cook the egg on low heat; scramble with the tips of 4 cooking chopsticks until tiny, uniform lumps are formed. Try to make the lumps as fine as possible. Remove from heat when cooked through; continue scrambling until fine, light lumps are formed.
5. Mix in the carrot and *shiitake* mushroom slices while the sushi rice is still warm. Turn out onto a flat-bottomed vessel (if you made the sushi rice using a sushi rice tub, just keep it in that); top with the minced egg and green peas.

* How to rehydrate dried *shiitake* mushrooms

Slowly rehydrating the dried *shiitake* mushrooms improves the taste. It also prevents the loss of nutrients. Soaking in water in the refrigerator for at least 24 hours is ideal. You do not need to worry about soaking them a little bit longer; 2 to 3 days is still okay, you can add water at anytime and put them in an airtight container so that you can use when you need. Refrigerated, they can be used at your convenience (however, they should be frozen after 3 days). When I open a bag of dried *shiitake* mushrooms, I rehydrate the whole bag. When they are nice and soft, I divide them in small portions, wrap them in plastic, and freeze them; or, I simmer them in soy sauce and sugar, divide them into portions, and then freeze them. You should treasure these. In an emergency, you can add just enough water to cover them, wrap in plastic, and microwave for a few minutes, but the flavor is not nearly the same. I strongly recommend

サケとイクラのちらし寿司

魚を使ったちらし寿司でも、スモークサーモンとイクラなら、どこでも手に入りやすく、買い置きも可能です。イクラはなくてもかまいません。スモークサーモンには生臭みがあるので、しその葉など香りのよい緑のものが加わると、味も見た目もぐんと引き立ちます。しそが手に入らなければ、バジルや香菜、ライムの皮のすりおろしなど、お好みのフレッシュハーブを散らしてみてください。

〈酢飯〉

米 …………2カップ
水 …………2カップ（酒を使う場合はここから大さじ2杯分の水を減らす）
酒 …………大さじ2（好みで）
昆布………3センチ角1枚（好みで）
すし酢……大さじ5（米酢大さじ4、砂糖大さじ1、塩小さじ1.5を溶けるまでまぜる）
しょうが…1かけ（できるだけ細かいみじん切りにしてすし酢にまぜておく）

〈具〉

スモークサーモン …………200g程度
イクラ………1パック（⅓カップ程度）
しその葉…4〜5枚

rehydrating the entire bagful and freezing what you do not use immediately.

Chirashi-zushi with salmon and salmon roe

If you want to make fish-based *chirashi-zushi*, using smoked salmon and salmon roe is a good choice because the ingredients are easy to find and they keep well. You do not need to use the salmon roe. Since smoked salmon has a bit of a fishy smell, use some green aromatics, such as *shiso*, to make it tastier and more visually appealing. If you have trouble getting your hands on *shiso*, you can use basil, coriander, or even the zest of lime; try using whatever fresh herbs you like.

Sushi rice
- 2 cups rice
- 2 cups water (if adding sake, reduce water by 2 tablespoons)
- 2 tablespoons sake (optional)
- 3-cm square piece of *konbu* (optional)
- 5 tablespoons sushi vinegar: 4 tablespoons rice vinegar, 1 tablespoon sugar, 1½ teaspoons salt, stirred in until dissolved
- 1 thumb-sized piece of ginger (minced as finely as possible and mixed with the sushi vinegar)

Ingredients
- 200 g smoked salmon
- 1 pack salmon roe (about ⅓ cup)
- 4 to 5 *shiso* leaves

1 しょうがのみじん切りをまぜたすし酢で酢飯をつくる（酢飯のつくり方は66ページ）。

2 冷めた酢飯を平たい器に盛り、食べやすい大きさに切ったサーモンを上に散らす。

3 イクラを小さじ1杯分くらいずつ、ところどころに置き、千切りにしたしその葉を散らす。

巻き寿司：ホームメイド寿司の上級編

　巻き寿司はアメリカのスシレストランのメイン商品です。といってもかんぴょう巻きやかっぱ巻きといったおなじみの巻き寿司でなく、アメリカの巻き寿司はとにかく派手で豪華です。カリフォルニアロールに始まって、ボストンロール（サケの皮入り）、フィラデルフィアロール（クリームチーズ入り）、スパイダーロール（ソフトシェルクラブの天ぷら巻き）などもはや定番。店の名や町の名をつけたオリジナルロールもよく見かけます。

　そうした具がいっぱいの豪華な巻き寿司も基本は同じ。巻き寿司をつくるにはちょっとしたコツと技術がいりますが、何回かつくるうちにうまく巻けるようになります。とはいえ、ちらし寿司や手巻き寿司のように最初から簡単にというわけにはいかないので、いわばホームメイド寿司の上級編です。

1. Prepare the sushi rice using the sushi vinegar with ginger mixed in (see page 67 for a detailed description of how to make sushi rice).
2. Spread the sushi rice out on a flat serving dish; cut the smoked salmon into bite-sized pieces and scatter on top of the rice.
3. Place the salmon roe on top of the rice with the salmon in 1-teaspoon-sized clusters; sprinkle the julienned *shiso* on top.

Sushi rolls—advanced home-made sushi

Sushi rolls are the most popular type of sushi on Japanese menus in the United States. That said, I am not talking about the gourd strip rolls or cucumber rolls that we Japanese are so familiar with; sushi rolls in the United States are flamboyant, sumptuous creations. Standard items include California rolls, Boston rolls (with salmon skin rolled in), Philadelphia rolls (with cream cheese), and spider rolls (with soft shelled crab tempura rolled in). You will often find creative sushi rolls named after the restaurant itself or the town that it is in.

These gorgeously filled sushi rolls are made no differently from ordinary ones. A little bit of skill—technique, if you will—is required to make sushi rolls, but you will get the hang of it if you keep trying. But, do not expect the same good results from the beginning that you may have had with *chirashi-zushi* or hand-rolled sushi. Sushi

まず巻きやすいかっぱ巻きから始めましょう。なれたら次はカリフォルニアロール。具が増えてもつくり方は同じですが、具が増えた分だけ酢飯の量も増やして広くひろげ、しっかり具を包みこむようにします。具が真ん中にならずに具が海苔に直接触れているところがあると、そこからくずれてきます。

かっぱ巻き（4本分）

酢飯…………茶碗2杯程度
きゅうり……1本
海苔…………2枚

＊酢飯は完全に冷めてしまうと堅くなって巻きにくくなります。少し温かみが残っている酢飯がベストです。

1. 小さいボウルに酢水（酢を水で半分に割ったもの）を用意する。海苔は半分に切っておく。
2. きゅうりを海苔の幅に合わせて細長く切る。日本のきゅうりなら1本を6つ割り程度、アメリカの太いきゅうりの場合は半分に割って種をスプーンでとってから巻きやすい太さに切る。
3. 巻きすに海苔を置く。海苔は巻き上がったときにつやのある面が出るように、つやのある面を下にする。手を酢水で湿らせ、茶碗に半分程度の酢飯を軽く握り、海苔の上に均等に押しつけるようにのばしていく。その際、海苔の向こう端は2センチ弱残しておく。
4. 酢飯の手前3分の1くらいのところに指先で軽く溝をつくっていき、そこに細く切ったきゅうりを置く。
5. 巻きすごと手前から持ち上げて、指先できゅうりを

rolls are about as advanced as you can get at home.

We will begin with the easier-to-roll *kappa-maki*. Once you have mastered that, we will move on to California rolls. They are rolled in the same way, but you have to spread out more sushi rice and make sure the additional fillings are rolled up firmly. They will fall apart if the fillings are not in the center and come in direct contact with the *nori*.

Kappa-maki (cucumber roll; makes 4 rolls)

2 bowlfuls sushi rice
1 cucumber
2 sheets *nori*

* Sushi rice becomes hard when it gets cold, making it difficult to roll; slightly warm sushi rice works best.

1. Mix some vinegar and water (50:50) in a small bowl. Cut sheets of *nori* in half.
2. Cut the cucumber lengthwise into sticks equal to the width of the *nori*. If you are using Japanese cucumbers, make about 6 sticks. Cucumbers in the United States are larger; cut them in half lengthwise, remove the seeds with a spoon, then cut them into easy-to-roll thicknesses.
3. Place *nori* sheet on bamboo mat. *Nori* has a shiny side, and it should be on the outside when rolled, so place the *nori* sheet shiny-side down on the mat. Dip fingers in vinegared water; grab about ½ bowlful of sushi rice and squeeze it gently into a shape about as long as the *nori* is wide. Spread it out evenly on the *nori*, leaving

おさえるようにしながら手前から向こうへしっかりと締めて巻いていく。最後まで巻けたら、海苔の合わせ目が下になるように回転させて、あらためて巻きすで巻いてしっかり締める。

⑥ 食べる直前に、包丁でひと口大に切る（1本を6切れくらい）。このとき1回切るごとにぬらした布巾（ふきん）かペーパータオルで包丁をふくようにするときれいに切れる。

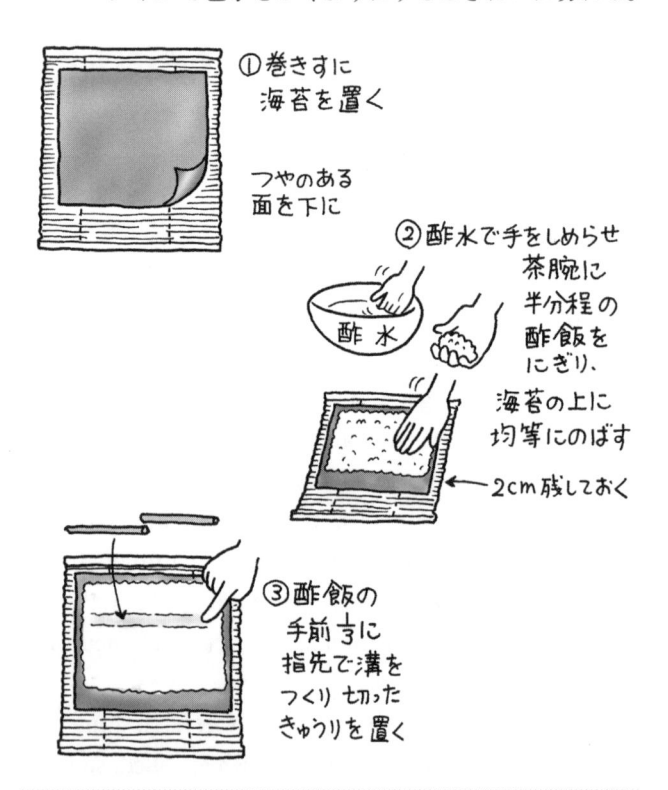

①巻きすに海苔を置く

つやのある面を下に

②酢水で手をしめらせ茶腕に半分程の酢飯をにぎり、海苔の上に均等にのばす

酢水

2cm残しておく

③酢飯の手前⅓に指先で溝をつくり切ったきゅうりを置く

---

1. Place *nori* sheet on bamboo mat. Make sure the shiny side is down.
2. Wet your hands with the vinegar/water solution. Take a handful (about ½ a rice bowl) of sushi rice, squeeze it, and spread it out on the *nori*. Leave 2 cm uncovered.
3. Form a grove with your fingers in the sushi rice about ⅓ of the way up and put the cucumber in it.

just under 2 cm of *nori* exposed on the far end.

4. About ⅓ of the way from the front of the sushi rice, make a groove by pressing down lightly with your fingers. Place the cucumber in the groove.
5. Starting from the edge closest to you, pick up the mat and roll firmly forward, using your other fingers to hold the cucumber in place. When you have completed rolling, a strip of *nori* should be left for a join. Turn so that the join is on the bottom. Roll again with the mat, pressing firmly.
6. Just before serving, slice with a knife into large pieces, roughly 6 to a roll. To make slicing easier, wipe the knife blade with a wet kitchen towel or wet paper towel after each pass of the blade.

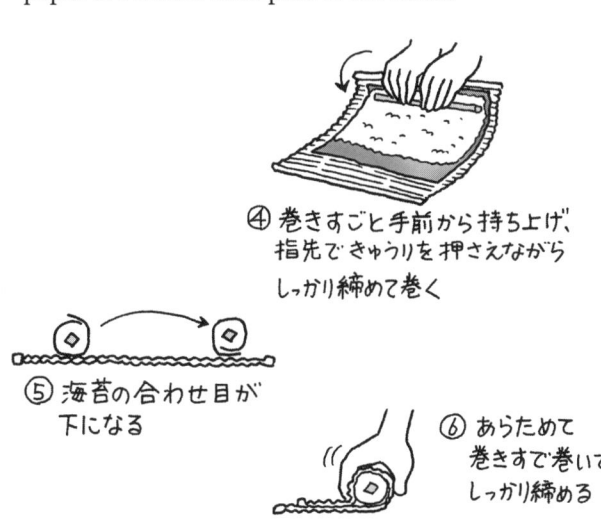

④ 巻きすごと手前から持ち上げ、指先できゅうりを押さえながらしっかり締めて巻く

⑤ 海苔の合わせ目が下になる

⑥ あらためて巻きすで巻いてしっかり締める

---

4. Pressing down on the cucumber with your fingers, lift the front side of the bamboo mat and roll firmly.
5. Make sure the uncovered part of the *nori* is on the bottom.
6. Using the bamboo mat, roll again, firmly.

裏巻きのカリフォルニアロール（2本分）

アメリカのスシレストランの巻き物には海苔(のり)が内側で酢飯が外側になった裏巻きが数多くあります。カリフォルニアロールも普通は裏巻きタイプです。真っ黒な海苔よりも赤いとびこや白いごまで覆われた裏巻きのほうが見た目が華やかだからでしょう。一見難しそうに見える裏巻きですが、実際に巻いてみると海苔を外側にする普通の海苔巻きよりも裏巻きのほうが初心者には巻きやすいことがわかります。かっぱ巻きがうまくできない方でも、裏巻きなら巻けることもあるので、挑戦してみてください。

酢飯が巻きすにくっつかないようにするためにはラップを使います。裏巻きの酢飯の外側につけるトッピングでもバリエーションが楽しめます。

酢飯……………茶碗2杯程度
海苔……………1枚
きゅうり………½本
アボカド………半分
カニかまぼこ…4本
ごま、またはとびこ

1. 巻きすにラップをひき、半分に切った海苔を置く（海苔の裏表はどちらでもよい）。
2. 酢水（同量の酢と水を混ぜたもの）に湿らせた手で茶碗1杯程度の酢飯を軽く握り、海苔に押しつける

Inside-out California rolls (makes 2 rolls)

There are many types of inside-out rolls—rolls with the *nori* on the inside and the sushi rice on the outside—in sushi restaurants throughout the United States. California rolls are usually prepared inside-out. This is most likely because the red flying fish roe and white sesame seeds are more colorful and pleasing to the eye when on the outside than plain black *nori*. At first sight these inside-out rolls may look difficult, but you will find that they are actually easier to roll for the beginner than ordinary sushi rolls. There are people who cannot handle rolling a cucumber roll, but can roll an inside-out roll, so give it a try.

Plastic wrap is used to keep the sushi rice from sticking to the bamboo mat. You can enjoy trying all sorts of toppings for the outside of the sushi rice.

2 bowlfuls sushi rice
1 sheet *nori*
½ of a cucumber
½ of an avocado
4 crab sticks
Sesame seeds or flying fish roe

1. Place a sheet of plastic wrap on the bamboo mat; place a half sheet of *nori* on it (do not worry which side is up).
2. Dip one hand in vinegared water (1 part vinegar to 1 part water) and use it to pick up about one bowlful

ように全体に均等に広げる。

3 ごま、またはとびこを広げた酢飯の上にふりかけて軽く押さえてから、海苔の両端を持って裏返す（酢飯がラップに接する側で海苔が上になる）。

4 海苔の手前3分の1くらいのところに細く切ったきゅうりとアボカド、カニかまぼこを置く。

5 具を指で押さえるようにしながら手前から向こうへ巻いていく。巻けたら、巻き終わり部分が下になるように回転させてから、あらためて巻きすでしっかり巻いて締める。

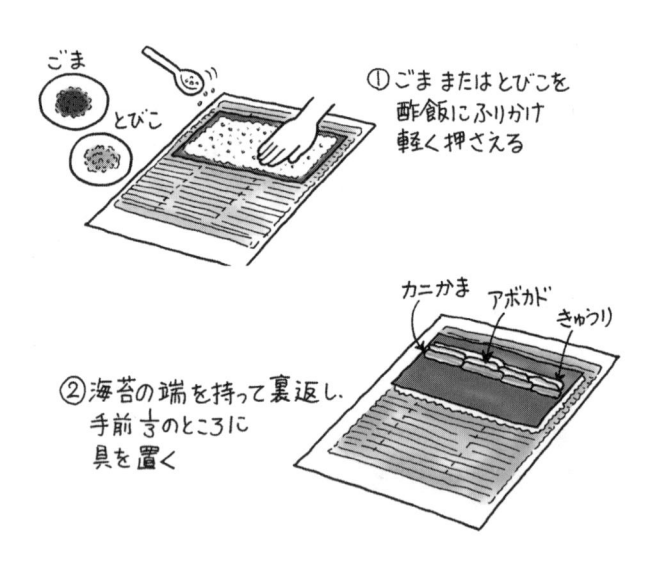

①ごま またはとびこを酢飯にふりかけ軽く押さえる

②海苔の端を持って裏返し、手前⅓のところに具を置く

---

1. Sprinkle sesame seeds or flying fish roe over the sushi rice and press down gently.
2. Grasp the edge of the *nori* and flip over. Place the fillings about ⅓ of the way up.

of sushi rice; squeeze gently. Spread sushi rice out evenly on the *nori*, pressing down lightly.

3. Sprinkle sesame seeds or flying fish roe over the sushi rice, pressing down on it lightly; pick up both edges of the *nori* and flip over, so the sushi rice is face-down on the plastic wrap.
4. Place thin strips of cucumber and avocado on *nori* about 1/3 of the way up; place crab sticks on top.
5. Pressing down on the fillings with your fingers, roll front to back. Turn the inside-out roll so that the join is on the bottom; roll tightly one more time.

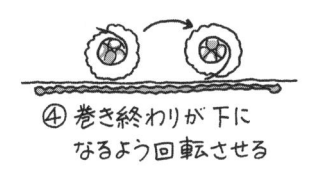

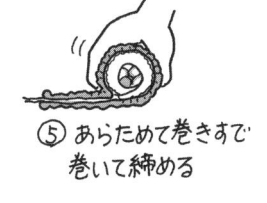

---

3. Pressing down firmly on the fillings, roll from front to back.
4. Turn the roll so that the seam is on the bottom.
5. Roll again, firmly.

3

汁物いろいろ麺類いろいろ
Soups and Noodles, Oodles and Oodles

出汁は日本料理の万能選手

　日本の汁物や煮物の基本は出汁。精進料理では昆布やしいたけの出汁を使いますが、一般的にはかつお節や煮干しが味の基本となります。肉や骨からとるスープストックが何時間もかかるのに比べ、調理時間5分以下という素早さでできるのでぜひお試しください。

　料亭の料理をつくるわけではありませんから、昆布やかつお節を入れたり引き上げたりするタイミングなど、細かいことにあまりこだわる必要はありません。かつお節を直接煮物に入れてそのまま食べてしまってもいいのです。昆布や煮干しも同様です。かつお節は、出汁をとるほかにも、料理のトッピングにしたり、炒め物にからめたり、さまざまに使えて便利です。

　かつお出汁でも煮干し出汁でも、冷蔵庫に保存するとすぐに味が落ちてしまいます。冷凍する方法もありますが、冷凍に必要な手間と場所を考えると、使うたびにつくったほうが能率がいいと思います。

Dashi—Japan's all-around player

Dashi is the basic stock used in Japanese soups and other boiled dishes. For vegetarian dishes, only *konbu* (kelp) and *shiitake* mushrooms are used to make the *dashi*, but generally, smoked dried bonito flakes (*katsuobushi*) and dried small sardines (*niboshi*) are used. Compared to stocks using meats and bones, which take hours to prepare, a good *dashi* can be whipped up in just 5 minutes.

Since we are not making food to be served at a traditional Japanese restaurant, we do not need to go on at length about the timing and other factors involved with adding and removing the *konbu* and bonito flakes. There is no reason why bonito flakes cannot be added to a boiled dish and eaten along with it. The same goes for the *konbu* and dried sardines. Bonito flakes are used for more than just flavoring *dashi*; they are convenient to use as toppings and can be added to stir-fried dishes. There really is no limit to their uses.

Both bonito flake *dashi* and dried sardine *dashi* can be stored in the refrigerator, but they lose their flavor quickly; alternatively, they can be frozen, but considering the effort involved, I find it is more efficient to make it each time you need it.

かつお節と昆布の出汁

水 …………………………… 4カップ
昆布………………………… 15センチ角くらい1枚
かつお節（削り節）…… 20g

1. 水と昆布を鍋に入れ、弱火にかける（時間があれば昆布はあらかじめ水に浸しておく）。
2. 沸騰しそうになったところで昆布を引き上げ、かつお節を入れます。
3. 再び沸騰したら弱火にし、数分煮てから火を止め、5分程度そのまま置く。
4. 目の細かいザルでこす（かつお節は最後にお玉などでギュッとしぼる）。

＊すぐに少量の出汁がほしいとき
少量の出汁がすぐに必要なときには、かつお節10g程度にカップ1杯の熱湯を注いで、2〜3分おいてから茶漉しなどでこします。かつお節はスプーンなどでギュッとしぼって出汁を出し切ります。

煮干し出汁

煮干しの出汁は味噌汁をはじめ、さまざまな料理に使えます。生臭くならないようにするポイントは、頭と腹

Bonito flake and *konbu dashi*

4 cups water
1 piece *konbu*, about 15-cm square
20 g bonito flakes

1. Put water and *konbu* in a saucepan; heat on low (if there is time, let the *konbu* soak in the water first).
2. Remove *konbu* just before water reaches a boil; add bonito flakes.
3. Lower heat when water reaches a boil; simmer for a few minutes, turn off heat, and let stand for 5 minutes.
4. Strain *dashi* through a fine strainer into another saucepan (use a ladle to press down on the bonito flakes remaining in the strainer to extract the liquid from them).

* When you need a little *dashi* in a hurry
When you are in a hurry and need just a little bit of *dashi*, pour a cup of boiling water on about 10 g of bonito flakes; let stand for 2 or 3 minutes before straining with a tea strainer or other utensil. Squeeze out that last bit of flavor by pressing down on the bonito flakes with a spoon.

Dried sardine *dashi*

Dried sardine *dashi* can be used in a variety of dishes, especially *miso* soups. To keep the *dashi* from smelling

の部分をあらかじめとっておくこと。煮干しもかつお節と同様、味噌汁や煮物に最初から直接入れて、一緒に食べてしまってもいいのです。

ただし、煮干しの魚まるごと1匹の形状は、小さいとはいえアメリカ人には敬遠されがち。まず、かつお出汁に慣れてからのほうがいいかもしれません。煮干しは酸化しやすいので、開封したら密閉容器や冷凍用ポリ袋に入れて冷凍庫に保存します。

水 ………… 4カップ
煮干し ……10匹程度

1. 煮干しはあらかじめ頭と腹の部分をとっておく。
2. 水に煮干しを入れて火にかけ、沸騰したら火を弱め、アクをとりながら5分程度煮る。時間があれば、煮干しはあらかじめ水に浸しておく。ひと晩おいたら翌朝はさっと煮立たせるだけでよい。

かつお節と煮干しvsだしのもとやめんつゆ

日本の多くの家庭の台所には、かつお節や煮干しとと

"fishy," remove the heads and stomach areas of the sardines before using them. As with the bonito flakes, you can add the dried sardines directly to the *miso* or other soup right from the beginning and eat them along with the rest of the ingredients.

However, even though the individual sardines are quite small, Americans will shy away from eating them whole. It is probably better to let them get used to just the *dashi* first. Dried sardines will react with oxygen if left exposed to air, so after opening a bag, put them in an air-tight container or freezer bag and store them in the freezer.

4 cups water
10 or so dried sardines

1. Remove heads and stomach areas of the sardines.
2. Put them in the water; heat. Lower heat when water reaches a boil; simmer 5 minutes and remove any scum from the surface. If there is time, let the dried sardines soak in the water before heating. If soaked overnight, all you have to do the next morning is bring them to a boil.

Bonito flake and dried sardine *dashi* vs. instant *dashi* and prepared noodle broth

In most Japanese kitchen cupboards you will find instant

もに、だしのもとやめんつゆも常備されていると思います。煮干しはなく、かつお節もトッピングぐらいにしか使わないという方も珍しくないかもしれません。出汁は日本料理の基本ではありますが、だしのもとやめんつゆは一切使わず、必ず自分で出汁をとるという日本人は、むしろ少数派でしょう。

外国人に日本の家庭料理を教えるにも、だしのもとやめんつゆはどんどん活用していいはずです。相手が外国人となると、つい本格的にやらなければ、と思いがちですが、日本人でさえめったにやらなくなっていることばかりを教えても敷居は高くなるばかり。私は、日本の出汁が何からできているのか、どうやってつくるのかを知ってもらうために出汁のとり方は教えますが、同時にだしのもとやめんつゆの使い方も紹介することにしています。

かつお節も本格的にするなら、使うたびに削るのが望ましいわけですが、そこまでいくと今や日常生活を超えた趣味の領域となってしまいます。かつお節削りも、削るかつお節自体も、簡単には手に入りません。かつお節はなるべく小さなパック入りの削り節をおすすめします。削り節は、封の切りたては香ばしい匂いがしますが、すぐに生臭さが出てきます。毎日たっぷりの出汁をとるならともかく、たまに使うのに大袋は向きません。また、煮干しも封を切ったら冷凍庫に保管して酸化を防ぎます。

dashi and a bottle of noodle broth next to the bonito flakes and dried sardines. But it is probably not unusual to find a few people who do not use the dried sardines and have only enough bonito flakes on hand for the occasional topping. While *dashi* may be the foundation for Japanese food, certainly those Japanese who never use instant *dashi* or prepared noodle broth, insisting on making their own *dashi*, are in the minority.

I think it is becoming more and more acceptable to include the use of instant *dashi* and prepared noodle broth when teaching foreigners how to make Japanese home-cooked meals. It is understandable that you want to teach a foreigner how to do something from scratch, the traditional way, but given the fact that even the Japanese are doing this less and less frequently, you are really just raising the threshold even higher. I teach foreigners how to make *dashi*, because I want them to know what it is and what ingredients are used. But, at the same time, I introduce them to instant *dashi* and prepared noodle broth.

To do bonito flakes properly, the dried bonito should be "shaved" each time you need the flakes. But going to that extreme these days is only for die-hard hobbyists, not the family cook. Finding both the dried bonito block and the utensil for shaving it is no easy task. I recommend bonito flakes sold in small packages. The flakes smell wonderful just after opening the package, but they soon take on a "fishy" odor. If you are going to be making lots of *dashi* every day, fine, but otherwise you should not buy bonito flakes in large

汁物のバリエーション：
味噌味のもの、塩・醤油味のもの

日本の汁物には、大きく分けて吸い物味（塩と醤油味）と味噌味があり、それぞれにかつお出汁を使う場合と煮干し出汁を使う場合があります。味噌汁はかつお出汁または煮干し出汁のどちらを使ってもかまいませんが、お吸い物にはかつお出汁を使います。また、精進料理のお吸い物やお味噌汁は昆布出汁が基本です。

味噌汁

味噌汁の具には野菜や大豆製品、貝類、海草などを組み合わせて使います。ここでは最も一般的な豆腐とわかめを使いましたが、季節に合わせていろいろお試しください。大根やきのこ類など堅い素材の場合には、だし汁が冷たいうちに入れて、やわらかくなるまで煮てから味噌を溶き入れます。また、貝類のお味噌汁に出汁は必要ありません。貝類を水から煮るとよい出汁が出ます。味噌の塩分はブランドや種類によってかなり違うので、味をみながら加減してください。

packages. And, for dried sardines, make sure they are stored in the freezer after opening to prevent them from reacting with oxygen.

Soup variations—they come in *miso* and salt/soy sauce flavors

Japanese soups can be broadly divided into the clear category (salt/soy sauce flavore) and the *miso* category. You will use bonito flake or dried sardine *dashi* on either, depending on the soup. For *miso* soup, you can use either bonito flake or dried sardine *dashi*, but for clear soups bonito flake *dashi* is used. For vegetarian, *miso* soup and clear soup, use a *konbu dashi*.

Miso soup

Miso soup consists of a variety of ingredients, such as vegetables and soy bean products, clams and other shell fish, and seaweed. Here we use tofu and *wakame*, a kind of seaweed, but try using anything in season. Firmer ingredients, such as *daikon* and mushrooms, should be added to cool *dashi* and simmered until soft before adding the *miso*. If you use clams or other shell fish, you do not need the *dashi*; they create their own *dashi* as they simmer. The salt content of *miso* varies by type and from brand to brand, so taste it as you use it.

出汁…………2カップ
味噌…………大さじ2〜3
豆腐…………½パック
わかめ………大さじ1（乾燥）

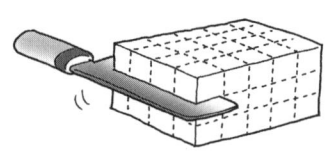

1 出汁を沸騰直前まで火にかけて温める。
2 豆腐をさいの目に切る。
3 豆腐とわかめを出汁に入れる。
4 味噌を溶いて、再び沸騰直前まで温める。

＊味噌汁の具の例
　根菜（大根、かぶ、たまねぎ、じゃがいも、さといも）
　野菜（ねぎ、小松菜、キャベツ、白菜、三つ葉）
　きのこ類（しいたけ、えのきだけ、しめじ、なめこ）
　貝・海藻類（アサリ、シジミ、わかめ）
　大豆製品（豆腐、油揚げ）
　乾物類（麩、切干大根）

豚汁

　これ1品にごはんとお漬物でもあれば食事になる、具だくさんの味噌汁。材料は、これがなければというものではありません。豚肉は必須ですが、あとは最低にんじんといも、ねぎがあれば豚汁らしくなります。もちろん材料がにぎやかになれば風味がより豊かになります。薬味に七味唐辛子をふってどうぞ。

2 cups *dashi*
2 to 3 tablespoons *miso*
½ pack tofu
1 tablespoon *wakame* (dried)

1. Heat *dashi* until almost boiling.
2. Cut tofu into cubes.
3. Add tofu and *wakame* to *dashi*.
4. Dissolve *miso* into *dashi*; heat again until almost boiling.

* *Miso* soup ingredients
Root vegetables (*daikon*, turnips, onions, potatoes, and taro)
Vegetables (scallions, Japanese mustard spinach, cabbage, Chinese cabbage, and *mitsuba*)
Mushrooms (*shiitake*, *enoki*, *shimeji*, and *nameko*)
Clams and seaweed (*asari* [Manila] clams, *shijimi* clams, and *wakame* seaweed)
Soy products (tofu and deep-fried bean curd)
Dry goods (dried wheat gluten and dried strips of *daikon*)

Tonjiru (pork and vegetable soup)

With a bowl of rice and some pickles, this is a meal in itself; the soup is quite substantial, given the large quantity and variety of ingredients. Other than pork, this soup requires no special ingredients. At the very least, add some carrots, potatoes, and scallions, and you have *tonjiru*. Of course, the wider the variety of ingredients,

出汁	4カップ
味噌	大さじ4〜6
豚肉（細切れ）	100グラム
野菜類	適宜(さといもまたはじゃがいも、にんじん、大根、ごぼう、しいたけ、こんにゃくなど)
豆腐	1/4丁
ねぎ	小口切りで好きなだけ（大さじ2程度）

1. 野菜はそれぞれひと口大以下の大きさに切っておく。こんにゃくは水からゆで、沸騰したら数分煮て、水を切ってから小さく切る。豆腐もさいの目に切っておく。ねぎ以外の具はすべて合わせて3カップ程度の量。ねぎは小口切りにしておく。

2. 鍋に少量の植物油を熱し、豚肉を炒める。
3. 出汁と味噌を加え、ねぎ以外の野菜、こんにゃくを入れ、野菜がやわらかくなるまで煮る。
4. 豆腐とねぎを加え、ひと煮立ちしたらでき上がり。

*こんにゃく
　蒟蒻芋といういもに含まれるコンニャクマンナンという多糖を固めた日本独特の加工食品。堅いゼリーのような歯ごたえと独特の香りがありますが、こんにゃく自体に味はあまりなく、主に歯ごたえを楽しむ食材です。超低カロリーで繊維質が豊富なので、ダイエットにいいとされています。汁物や和え物に入れると味に変化が出ていいものですが、その正体のわからなさ故に、初めて食

the more elaborate the dish becomes. For seasoning, try some Japanese seven-spice mix.

4 cups *dashi*
4 to 6 tablespoons *miso*
100 g pork (thinly sliced and cut into small pieces)
Vegetables as desired (taro, potatoes, carrots, *daikon*, burdock root, *shiitake* mushrooms, *konnyaku*, etc.)
¼ block tofu
Chopped scallions to taste (about 2 tablespoons)

1. Cut all the vegetables into bite-size or smaller pieces. Place *konnyaku* in water and bring to a boil; simmer for a few minutes, strain, and cut into small pieces. Cut the tofu into cubes. Excluding the scallions, you should have about 3 cups of ingredients. Slice scallions finely.
2. Heat a small amount of oil in a saucepan; fry pork.
3. Add *dashi*, *miso*, all vegetables except for scallions, and *konnyaku*; simmer until vegetables are soft.
4. Add tofu and scallions; simmer briefly.

* *Konnyaku* (konjac)
Konnyaku is a special Japanese processed food utilizing solidified konjac mannan, a plant polysaccharide, extracted from konjac rhizomes. While it has the bite of a hard jelly and a fragrance all its own, it has very little taste; it is mostly the texture that is appreciated. Considered a good food for dieters, it contains a lot of fiber but very few calories. It can transform the taste

べる外国人にはちょっと勇気がいるようです。

お吸い物

出汁に塩と少量の醤油(しょうゆ)だけで味をつけるお吸い物は、出汁(だし)の味が大切なので、ぜひかつ節の出汁を使ってください。季節の具を彩りよく入れるのもポイントです。魚介類などを主な具にして、野菜、柚子(ゆず)や三つ葉など、香りのあるものを合わせます。あらかじめ火を通した具を形よく碗に盛ってから熱い出汁を注ぎます。出汁の味つけはあくまでも目安ですので、好みで加減してください。

出汁………2カップ
塩 ………小さじ½
醤油………小さじ1

かき玉汁

出汁(だし)と卵だけで簡単にできる、お吸い物よりも少しカジュアルなおつゆです。

出汁………2カップ
塩 ………小さじ1/2
醤油………小さじ1
片栗粉(かたくりこ)……小さじ1(大さじ1の水でといておく)

of soups and mixed dishes, but for the foreigner who knows little about it, it takes a bit of courage to eat it for the first time.

Osuimono (clear soups)

Osuimono uses only salt and a small amount of soy sauce in the *dashi*, so you should use a bonito flake *dashi*, as it is integral to the overall taste. It is also important to use colorful ingredients that are in season. Seafood is usually the main ingredient, but the flavor is complemented with vegetables and aromatics, such as *yuzu* zest and *mitsuba*. Cook the ingredients in advance and assemble them in the bowl before adding the hot *dashi*. The following suggestions for the *dashi* are just that, suggestions, so adjust the seasonings according to your own taste.

2 cups *dashi*
½ teaspoon salt
1 teaspoon soy sauce

Eggdrop soup

All you need is dashi and eggs. It is a very casual type of soup.

2 cups *dashi*
½ teaspoon salt
1 teaspoon soy sauce
1 teaspoon cornstarch (mixed in 1 tablespoon water)

卵 ………… 1個

1. 出汁に調味料を入れて煮立て、かきまぜながら水溶き片栗粉をいれてとろみがつくまで煮る。

2. とろみがついたら、よく溶いた卵を回し入れながらかきまぜる。再び煮立ったらでき上がりです。

けんちん汁

ベジタリアンにもおすすめできる具沢山の精進汁です。豆腐と油揚げはぜひ入れたい具材ですが、野菜はあるもので結構です。

出汁 ……… 4カップ
塩 ………… 小さじ1
醤油 …… 小さじ2
豆腐 ……… ½丁
油揚げ ….. 1枚
野菜類 …. 適宜（にんじん、大根、ごぼう、しいたけ、こんにゃくなど）
ねぎ ……… 小口切りで好きなだけ（大さじ2程度）
ごま油 …. 小さじ1

1. 野菜はそれぞれひと口大以下の大きさに切っておく。こんにゃくは水からゆで、沸騰したら数分煮て水を切ってから小さく切る。豆腐はさいの目、油揚げは細切りにしておく。ねぎ以外の具はすべて合わせて3カップ程度。ねぎは小口切り。

1 egg

1. Add seasoning to *dashi* and bring to boil; add the cornstarch mixed in water, stirring continuously, and simmer until thickened.
2. Once thickened, slowly stir in a well beaten egg; return to boil, turn off heat.

Kenchin soup

This is a wonderful vegetarian dish with lots of ingredients. You should be sure to add tofu and deep-fried bean curd, but for the vegetables you can use whatever is handy.

4 cups *dashi*
1 teaspoon salt
2 teaspoons soy sauce
½ block tofu
1 piece deep-fried bean curd
Vegetables, as desired (Use carrots, *daikon*, burdock root, *shiitake* mushrooms, *konnyaku*, etc.)
Scallions, as desired, thinly sliced (about 2 tablespoons)
1 teaspoon sesame oil

1. Cut all the vegetables into, bite-size or smaller pieces. Place *konnyaku* in water and bring to a boil; simmer for a few minutes, strain, and cut into small pieces. Cut the tofu into cubes. Cut the deep-fried bean curd into thin slices. Excluding the scallions,

2 鍋にごま油を熱し、豆腐を炒める。
3 水が出てきてもそのまま炒め続け、ねぎ以外の材料を加えてさらに炒める。
4 出汁と調味料を入れ野菜がやわらかくなるまで煮たら、ねぎをくわえてひと煮立ちさせる。

麺類のバリエーション

　日本の麺類の代表的なものといえば、うどんとそば。ほかに家庭でよく食卓に上る麺類といえば、そうめんです。いずれも冷たいつけ麺としても、温かい汁麺としても手軽に料理できます。最近は、うどんは冷凍も多く出回っていますが、世界中どこでもつくれるとなると乾麺です。日本の乾麺がなく、和風の麺が食べたいというときには極細パスタのカッペリーニをそうめん代わりに使ってみてください。冷たくしても、温かいにゅう麺でもおいしく食べられます。

　めんつゆはつくりおきして好みの濃さに薄めて使えます。もちろん市販のめんつゆを使えば、さらに簡単にできます。

　麺類は具や薬味で、バリエーションがいくらでもききます。たんぱく質系の具と青味野菜をとり合わせれば、栄養のバランスもとれます。

you should have about 3 cups of ingredients. Slice scallions finely.
2. In a saucepan, heat the sesame oil; fry tofu.
3. Continue frying even if the tofu releases water; add all other ingredients except scallions.
4. Add *dashi* and seasonings; simmer until vegetables are soft. Add scallions; bring to boil for a moment, turn off heat.

Variations using noodles

Udon and *soba* are Japan's most famous noodle varieties. Another one that is often eaten at home is *somen*. They can all be easily served cold and dipped in a sauce when eating, or served hot in a soup. These days, we see a lot of frozen *udon*, but what you will find all over the world is the dried variety. When you cannot find any dried Japanese noodles, but the craving for them will not subside, try using angel hair pasta such as cappellini as a substitute for *somen*. They are fine cold, or hot as *nyumen*.

You can make the broth for noodles in advance and thin it to taste as necessary. Of course, it is even easier to use store-bought noodle broth.

There are an unlimited number of variations when combining different types of noodles and other ingredients and seasonings. Ingredients high in protein, along with green vegetables, make noodle soup a well balanced meal.

乾麺のゆで方

うどん、そば、そうめんなど、乾麺のゆで方の基本は同じです。大きな鍋にたっぷりのお湯でゆでること、途中で差し水をすること、ゆで上がってから水にさらすことがポイントとなります。

まず、大きめの鍋でお湯を沸騰させ、差し水用の水をコップに入れて用意しておきます。乾麺をパラパラとばらすように入れて、くっつかないように箸でかきまぜます。沸騰して吹きこぼれそうになったら、用意しておいた差し水を一気に入れてお湯の温度を下げます。すぐに次の差し水を用意して、再び沸騰したら、また差し水を入れます。その後は、吹きこぼれない程度に火を弱めて、麺がやわらかくなるまでゆでます。ゆで時間は麺の太さによるので、パッケージの説明をもとに好みのやわらかさを確かめながら決めてください。

①大きめの鍋にお湯を沸騰させ、乾麺をパラパラとバラすように入れくっつかないよう箸でかきまぜる。

差し水を用意する

②沸騰して吹きこぼれそうになったら差し水を一気に入れる。次の差し水を用意する

---

1. Bring a large pot of water to a boil. Spread out the dried noodles as you put them in the boiling water, making sure they do not stick together. Get a cup of water ready.
2. When the water returns to a boil and threatens to boil over, add the water.

Cooking dried noodles

The basic principle for cooking dried noodles is the same for *udon*, *soba*, and *somen*. The key is to use a large pot of water, add water part way through cooking, and rinse with water when done.

First, bring a large pot of water to a boil. Keep a cup of water handy too add part way through cooking. Separate the noodles as you drop them into the boiling water; to keep the noodles from sticking together, stir with chopsticks. When the water returns to a boil and threatens to boil over, add the cup of water to lower the temperature; get another cup of water ready for the same purpose. When it boils up again, add the water. If it looks like it will boil over a third time, lower the heat just enough to keep it at a rolling boil until the noodles are tender. Cooking times depend on the thickness of the noodles, so refer to the suggested cooking time printed on the package and check for tenderness as you cook.

③再び沸騰したら また差し水を入れる

④吹きこぼれない程度に火を弱めて麺がやわらかくなるまでゆでる

3. Repeat this once more when the water comes to a boil.
4. Lower the heat just enough to keep the water from boiling over; cook until soft.

ゆで上がったら水にさらしてぬめりをとります。冷たいつけ麺なら水を切ってそのまま、温かい汁麺ならよく水を切ってから熱い汁に入れて温めます。

3 冷たいそば（うどん）

めんつゆ（つけ汁）

さまざまに使える万能のつゆのもと。好みの濃さに薄めて使います。つけつゆで4倍程度が目安です。保存は冷蔵庫で、できるだけ早く使いきってください。

醤油1カップ、みりん1カップを煮立て、かつお節20gを入れて弱火で数分煮る。火をとめて5分ほど置いてからこす。

ごまダレ

ちょっとこってりした味がそうめんに特によく合います。うどんにもおすすめします。

好みの濃さに水で薄めためんつゆ半カップあたり、大さじ1のすりごまをまぜる。練りごま小さじ1を入れるとさらに濃厚な味になる。

冷たい麺類に合う薬味

冷たい麺類には、つけ汁に薬味を加えて味に変化をつけます。最低でも1種類、好みに合わせて何種類かを組

When the noodles are done, drain and rinse thoroughly to prevent them from sticking together. Noodles to be eaten cold should be rinsed and left to drain; if the noodles are to be eaten in a hot soup, add to the hot broth after rinsing well.

Cold *soba* (or *udon*)

Noodle broth (Dipping sauces)
This is marvelously useful for a variety of dishes. Dilute to taste, usually 1 part broth to 4 parts water. Store in the refrigerator, but try to use it up as quickly as possible.

> Combine 1 cup soy sauce and 1 cup *mirin*; bring to boil. Add 20 g bonito flakes and simmer on low for a few minutes. Turn off heat, let stand for 5 minutes strain.

Sesame sauce (dipping sauces)
The rich taste of sesame sauce especially suits *somen*. I recommend it for *udon*, too.

> Add about 1 tablespoon ground sesame seeds for every ½ cup of noodle broth which you have diluted to taste. For an even richer taste, add 1 teaspoon sesame paste.

Condiments for cold noodles
Condiments transform the taste of a dipping sauce for cold noodles. You should use at least one of the condi-

み合わせてもいいでしょう。

わさび
さらしねぎ(ねぎを薄く小口切りにして水にさらして水気をしぼったもの)
おろししょうが
大根おろし
ごま
しその葉の千切り
海苔の細切り

冷たい麺類に合う具

天ぷら
かまぼこ(薄切りか千切り)
きゅうりの千切り
かいわれ大根
蒸し鶏(細く割いておく)

温かい汁そば(うどん)

温かい麺のつゆ

　温かい麺類は具だくさんのスープのようなものですか

ments listed below, but combinations of them can be used to taste.

Wasabi
Sarashi-negi (scallions that have been thinly sliced, rinsed with water, and squeezed dry)
Grated ginger
Grated *daikon*
Sesame seeds
shiso, finely sliced
Nori, finely sliced

Ingredients for cold noodles

Tempura
Kamaboko (pureed and steamed fish loaf), thin or fine slices
Finely sliced cucumber
Daikon sprouts
Steamed chicken (finely shredded)

Soba (or *udon*) in a hot soup

Hot noodle broth

Hot noodle soups have a lot of ingredients, so they

ら、冷たい麺のつけ汁より味はずっと薄くつけます。味つけは好みですが、うどんには塩と少量の醤油で濃い目のお吸い物のような味、そばにはお醤油とみりんのきいた味つけが合うと思います。そうめんを温かく食べるにゅうめんもおいしいものです。にゅうめんの出汁はうどんと同じ塩味系がおすすめです。

味噌汁より濃い目に味つけして煮込んだ味噌煮込みうどんも体が温まります。

以下は味つけの目安ですので、好みによって加減してください。

温かいうどんの汁
出汁………2カップ
塩…………小さじ1
醤油………小さじ2
みりん……大さじ1

温かいそばの汁
出汁………2カップ
醤油………大さじ2
みりん……大さじ2

温かい麺類に合う薬味
きざみねぎ（ねぎを薄い小口切りにしてたっぷりと）
柚子（小さくそいだ皮をそえます）
七味唐辛子

do not need to be nearly as heavily seasoned as a cold dipping sauces. Season to taste, but, in general, salt and a dash of soy sauce with *udon* makes a deep, rich soup, and soy sauce and *mirin* go well with *soba*. *Somen* is tasty served as hot *nyumen*. For the *nyumen*, I recommend the same salt flavored *dashi* used for *udon*.

A bowl of *udon* simmered in a *miso*-based stock, somewhat stronger in taste than *miso* soup, will warm you up on a cold day.

The following suggestions for flavorings are just that, suggestions, so adjust accordingly to your own taste.

Soup for hot *udon*

2 cups *dashi*
1 teaspoon salt
2 teaspoons soy sauce
1 tablespoon *mirin*

Soup for hot *soba*

2 cups *dashi*
2 tablespoons soy sauce
2 tablespoons *mirin*

Condiments for hot noodle soups

Thinly sliced scallions; lots of them
Yuzu zest, finely sliced
Japanese seven-spice mix

温かい麺類に合う具

天ぷら

はんぺん

かまぼこ

鶏肉

油揚げの甘辛煮(油揚げ2枚をお湯で2〜3分煮て油抜きをし、お湯は捨てる。醤油大さじ2、みりん大さじ2、砂糖大さじ1に油揚げがかぶるくらいの水を加えて弱火で汁気が少なくなるまで煮る)

青菜(小松菜、ほうれんそう、水菜など)

もち(こんがり焼いてから入れる)

卵(溶いた卵を熱い汁に流し入れてかきまぜる。一緒に入れる具はねぎが合う)

Ingredients for hot noodle soups

Tempura

Hanpen (pureed and steamed fish, similar to *kamaboko*)

Kamaboko

Chicken

Deep-fried bean curd simmered in salty-sweet sauce (Simmer 2 sheets of deep-fried bean curd in hot water for 2 to 3 minutes to remove some of the oil; discard hot water. Add 2 tablespoons soy sauce, 2 tablespoons *mirin*, 1 tablespoon sugar, and enough water to cover the bean curd; simmer on low until most of the liquid evaporates)

Green-leaf vegetables (Japanese mustard spinach, spinach, and *mizuna*, etc.)

Mochi (pounded and shaped glutinous rice—grill it until it becomes golden brown before adding)

Egg (beat egg; slowly stir into hot soup—scallions go well with this)

4

日本流野菜料理
Cooking with Vegetables
—Japanese-Style

日本の家庭料理では、必ず1品は野菜料理が加わるのが普通です。調理や味つけは簡単ですが、野菜料理があると食卓がぐっと豊かになります。いずれも日本料理以外のメニューのサイドディッシュとしてもおすすめです。

4 切るだけの料理

日本流野菜料理

切るだけで、野菜の味を生で味わう日本流サラダ。単純な味つけですが、切り方ひとつで野菜の味わいが変わります。トントンと軽快な音を立てて野菜を切るのは楽しいものですが、包丁が苦手でも道具を使って簡単にできます。

早漬け

塩を使って野菜の味を引き出す一番簡単な料理です。食べやすい大きさに切って、塩をまぶし重しをしておくだけ。時間のないときには材料を薄く切って、塩でもむだけでもそれなりにおいしくなります。野菜が塩によってよい具合に脱水され自然な甘味が出てきます。塩だけでなく柚子や唐辛子、細かく切った昆布などを加えるとさらに風味が増します。

There is usually at least 1 vegetable dish at every meal served in a Japanese home. They are easy dishes to prepare and add an appealing richness to the dinner table. All of them make wonderful side dishes for any type of cuisine.

Just-cut cooking

A Japanese-style salad composed solely of sliced vegetables is a treat for your senses. The method of slicing transforms the flavors of the vegetables. The rhythmical "chop, chop, chop" when slicing the vegetables with a knife is very pleasant, but if you are not handy with a one then you can use other slicing utensils to easily do the job.

Haya-zuke (quick pickling)

This is the simplest method of bringing the flavor out of vegetables, using only salt. Just cut the vegetables into easy-to-eat pieces, sprinkle with salt, and place something heavy on it. When you do not have enough time, just slice the vegetables thinly, sprinkle with salt, amd rub it in gently. They will still be quite tasty. When the vegetables have been salted and release liquid nicely, they become naturally sweet. They are further enhanced by adding *yuzu* zest, chili pepper, or even thin slices of *konbu*.

野菜………(小さく切って2カップ程度)
塩…………小さじ1
好みで昆布（小さく切る）、柚子、唐辛子など

1. 野菜は生で食べられるものなら何でもよく、きゅうり、かぶ、大根、白菜が特におすすめ。1種類でも何種類もまぜてもかまいません。きゅうりはひと口大の乱切り、かぶや大根は薄切り（形は好みで）、白菜は葉の長いほうを3分の1に切ってから、それぞれを繊維に沿って、縦に太めの千切りに。

2. ボウルに野菜を入れて塩をまぶして軽くもんだら（昆布や唐辛子などを入れる場合には、一緒にもみ込む）、バネ式のプラスチックの漬物器に入れて蓋をして冷蔵庫にひと晩置く。100円ショップでも手軽に買える漬物器が1つあると便利。漬物器がない場合はお皿やボウルなどを使って重しをする。たとえば、少し小さめの別のボウルを野菜の上に重ね、その中に缶詰など、重しになるようなものを入れてから全体をラップで包む。

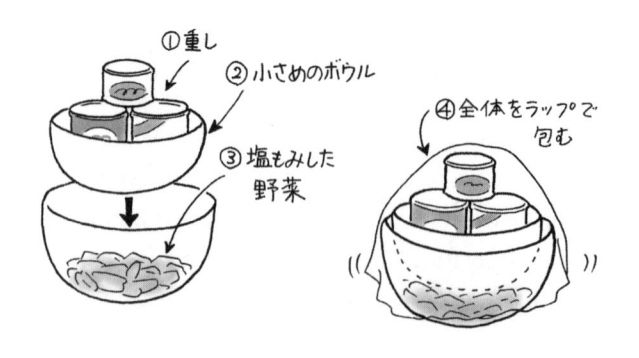

Vegetables (about 2 cups cut in small pieces)
1 teaspoon salt
Yuzu zest, chili pepper, or thin slices of *konbu*, as desired

1. Any vegetables that can be eaten raw will work fine. Some good examples are cucumbers, turnips, *daikon*, and Chinese cabbage. You can use just one type of vegetable, or mix as many types as you like. Chop cucumbers coarsely into bite-size pieces. Turnips and *daikon* should be sliced thinly (the shape is entirely up to you). Cut long Chinese cabbage leaves in thirds, then slice them into thin strips along the grain.
2. Place vegetables in a bowl; sprinkle with salt and rub gently (if you are adding *konbu*, chili peppers, etc., rub them in as well). Place in a spring-loaded plastic pickling press; cover and refrigerate overnight. A pickling press is very handy to have in your kitchen and can be purchased at 100 yen shops (where every item is about $1). If you do not have a pickling press, use a plate, bowl, or other object as a weight. For instance, you could place a slightly smaller bowl on top of the vegetables, put a can of tuna or other such weight into it, and cover the whole lot with plastic wrap.

---

1. Weights
2. Smaller bowl
3. Vegetables rubbed with salt
4. Cover with plastic wrap

醤油漬け

早漬けのバリエーションです。醤油とごま油でちょっと中華風の味になります。

きゅうり……1本
漬け汁（A）
　酢…………大さじ1杯
　醤油………大さじ1杯
　みりん……大さじ1杯
　ごま油……小さじ1杯
　唐辛子……少々（好みで）

1. きゅうりはひと口大の乱切りにする。
2. (A)の材料をすべて合わせた漬け汁で、きゅうりを漬け込む。漬けてすぐ食べられるが、2～3時間おくと味がしみてさらにおいしくなる。

きゅうりもみ

日本風きゅうりサラダです。ごく薄く切ったきゅうりを塩でもんでしんなりさせ、合わせ酢をかけます。原理は早漬けと同じですが、その切り方で独特の味わいになります。合わせ酢をかけて時間をおくと水っぽくなるので、和えるのは食べる直前に。

きゅうり……1本
塩……………小さじ¼

Shoyu-zuke (pickling in soy sauce)

This is a variation on *haya-zuke*. soy sauce and sesame oil give the vegetables a Chinese taste.

1 cucumber
Pickling liquid (A)
    1 tablespoon vinegar
    1 tablespoon soy sauce
    1 tablespoon *mirin*
    1 teaspoon sesame oil
    Chili pepper (optional)

1. Chop cucumbers coarsely into, bite-sized pieces.
2. Combine pickling liquid (A) ingredients; add cucumber. You can eat immediately, but it is better to let the cucumber stand in the liquid for 2 to 3 hours.

Kyuri-momi (cucumbers in a vinegar dressing)

This is a Japanese-style cucumber salad. Thin slices of cucumber are softened by rubbing salt in; a vinegar dressing is later poured over them. The theory is the same as with *haya-zuke*, but the slicing technique imparts a particular flavor. Pour the dressing on the cucumber slices just before serving; otherwise, they will become watery.

1 cucumber
¼ teaspoon salt

合わせ酢（A）
　すし酢（すし酢のつくり方は66ページ）…大さじ１
　醬油……小さじ¼

1. きゅうりをスライサーなどでごく薄切りにし、塩でもんでしんなりさせる。
2. きゅうりの水気をよくしぼり、(A)の材料をまぜた合わせ酢で和える。

大根おろし

　大根をおろし金でおろすだけのことですが、大根の最高の食べ方の１つです。昔から、胃の調子を整えるのにいいことでも知られています。麺類や鍋物の薬味としても欠かせないほか、焼き魚や焼き肉にも合います。海苔とかつお節と醬油をかければ、ごはんのおかずにもぴったり。

　同じ大根でも葉に近いほうほど甘みがあってまろやかで、しっぽはピリッとした辛味がありますから、用途に合わせて選びます。

包丁修行は「ネコの手」から

　菜っ切り包丁でリズミカルに切るきゅうりの薄切りは

Vinegar dressing (A)

1 tablespoon sushi vinegar (see page 67 for instructions)

¼ teaspoon soy sauce

1. Slice the cucumber as thinly as possible using a slicer or other kitchen utensil; rub salt in.
2. Squeeze out the cucumber's excess water; toss with vinegar dressing.

Grated *daikon*

Though simply a matter of grating *daikon* with a grater, it is one of the finest ways to eat *daikon*. It has also long been known as a remedy for an upset stomach. In addition to being an invaluable condiment for noodles and one-pot meals, it goes well with grilled fish and meat. Put a little bit of *nori* or bonito flakes on top, add a dash of soy sauce, and you have a perfect accompaniment for rice.

The same *daikon* root has a different flavor depending on which part you use. The closer to the leaves, the sweeter and milder the taste; the tail end has quite a sharp taste, so choose accordingly.

Knife training begins with "the paw of the cat"

In Japan, using a *nakiri bocho* (a Japanese knife for

日本では格別珍しいことではありませんが、アメリカ人の前でやると、まず確実に感心されます。日本流の包丁の使い方を覚えてもらうときにまず伝えるのは「ネコの手」。千切りなどをコントロールするのは材料を支えている左手ですが、指を切らないようにするには指を丸め込んで押さえる「ネコの手」スタイルをマスターすることが不可欠です。

包丁がよく切れることと、ある程度の大きさがあることも必要で、切れ味の悪いフルーツナイフで千切りをするのは不可能です。アメリカにはまな板もめったに使わない人が少なくないので、私は大人でも、材料を切るときにはまず包丁の基本を教えることにしています。

それでも、包丁使いがすぐにうまくなるわけではないので、薄切りにはスライサーを使いましょう。調子に乗って何でもかんでも包丁で切ってみせると、難しくてできないと思われてしまいます。

ゆでたり煮たり

葉野菜はサラダではなく、ゆでてからおひたしや和えものにするのが日本の伝統的な食べ方です。野菜はゆでると生よりもたっぷりの量が食べられます。ほうれん草

cutting vegetables) to rhythmically cut thin slices of cucumber raises few eyebrows. Do it in front of Americans, though, and they will watch you, thoroughly engrossed. When teaching them how to use Japanese knives, I first advise them about "the paw of the cat." When julienning or performing other tasks with a knife, the material you are cutting needs to be controlled with the left hand, but you have to make sure that your fingers are gently curled in the shape of a cat's paw in order to avoid injury.

In addition to being sharp, the knife needs to be large enough; do not try to cut vegetables with a dull small fruit knife. Since there are Americans who rarely use a cutting board, I begin by instructing them, even adults, in the basic method of using a knife.

But, even so, nobody gets really good at using a knife very quickly, so we might as well use a slicer. If you get too carried away cutting up all sorts of things with the knife, you might make them think that it is too difficult to learn.

Boiling and simmering

Greens are not used in salads; they are boiled first and served as *ohitashi* or dressed. That is the traditional way of eating them. Compared with eating them raw, you

のようにアクの強い野菜の場合、ゆでることによってアクを抜く効果もあります。

野菜をゆでるときに一番気をつけたいのがゆですぎです。ゆですぎた野菜は味も歯ごたえも損なわれます。ぐつぐつ煮るのではなく、さっと火を通すつもりでゆでてください。葉物ならしんなりすればゆで上がりです。

おひたし

ゆでて醤油味の出汁にひたすだけのことですが、葉物の最もおいしい食べ方の1つです。ほうれん草が最も一般的ですが、クレソンなど香りのある葉物だと大人の味になります。おひたしは味をつけずに各自が食卓で醤油をかける場合もありますが、出汁で割った醤油で和えたほうがおいしいと思います。めんつゆで和えてもおいしいです。薄めに味をつけて、塩味が物足りない方には醤油をかけてもらうようにします。

ほうれん草……1把（クレソンでも可）
合わせ醤油（A）
　醤油…………大さじ1
　出汁…………50㎖
かつお節またはすりごま………少々

1 ほうれん草はよく洗う。
2 大きめの鍋にたっぷりのお湯を沸かして塩大さじ1

can eat a lot more of them when they are boiled. Greens such as spinach contain a lot of impurities; boiling them has the added effect of releasing these impurities as scum and foam.

When boiling greens, be very careful not to overcook them. Overcooked greens lose their flavor and become mushy. Do not boil them gently; try to cook them through as quickly as possible. Leafy greens are ready when they become wilted.

Ohitashi

This dish is simply boiled leafy greens with a soy sauce *dashi* poured over them, but it is one of the greatest ways to eat these greens. Spinach is the standard leafy green used, but you can also use watercress or other fragrant greens for a more "adult" taste. Sometimes *ohitashi* is served just boiled and you add soy sauce to it at the table, but it is more delicious when you use soy sauce diluted with *dashi*. It is also good with noodle broth. Flavor lightly; your guests can always add soy sauce at the table.

1 bunch spinach (or watercress)
soy sauce mix (A)
   1 tablespoon soy sauce
   50 ml *dashi*
Just a touch of bonito flakes or ground sesame seeds

1. Wash spinach thoroughly.
2. Bring plenty of water to a boil in a large pot; add 1

を加える。

3 ほうれん草を鍋に一気に入れて全体がお湯にひたるようにかき回し、全体がしんなりしたらザルにあけて、たっぷりの冷水につける。こうすることで葉の緑が鮮やかになる。

4 ほうれん草の水気をよくしぼって食べやすい長さに切る。

5 （A）の材料をまぜた合わせ醬油をかけて、よくまぜ、かつお節またはすりごまをふりかける。

ごま和え

ほうれん草やクレソンなどの葉物でもおいしくつくれますが、材料がどこでも手に入って子供にも好評なのがいんげんのごま和えです。アスパラガスでも同様につくれます。

```
さやいんげん……300g
和えごろも（A）
  醬油……………大さじ2
  みりん…………大さじ2
  すりごま………大さじ2杯
```

1 いんげんはスジをとって、食べやすい長さに折り、鍋に入れる。鍋にいんげんが半分かぶるくらいの水を入れ、蓋をして強火にかける。

2 煮立ったら火を弱め、1分ほどで火からおろし、ザルにあけて冷ます。このとき水にさらすと水っぽくなってしまうので、ザルをふって熱をとばすようにする。

tablespoon salt.

3. Add all the spinach to the pot at once and stir, making sure the spinach is submerged. Drain in a strainer when wilted; rinse with plenty of cold water. This will help the spinach retain its dark green color.
4. Squeeze out water and cut spinach to desired length.
5. Pour the soy sauce mix (A) over the spinach and mix well; sprinkle with bonito flakes or sesame seeds.

Sesame dressing

A sesame dressing is great with spinach, watercress, and other leafy greens, but here we use green beans because they are easy to find and kids love them. The recipe is the same for asparagus.

300 g green beans
Sesame dressing (A)
    2 tablespoons soy sauce
    2 tablespoons *mirin*
    2 tablespoons ground sesame seeds

1. Trim green beans and snap into bite-sized lengths; place in pot. Add water to cover about half the beans; cover, heat on high.
2. Bring to a boil; lower heat, simmer for 1 minute. Remove from heat, drain in strainer, cool. Rinsing in cold water would make the beans too watery, so cool by tossing them in the air with the strainer.

③ (A)をすべてまぜた和えごろもを、ゆでたいんげんにまぜる。いんげんは完全に冷めていなくてもかまわないが、食べる直前に和えるようにする。

＊海外などで、すりごまが簡単に手に入らない場合には、生のごまからつくります。天板になるべく重ならないようにごまをしきつめ、摂氏180度（華氏350度）で、ところどころきつね色になるまで焼きます（2〜3分）。香ばしくなったごまをすり鉢でするか、フードプロセッサーにかけて細かく砕きます。フードプロセッサーを使う場合、長くかけすぎると油が出てきて練りごまになってしまうので、まだサラッとした状態のうちに止めます。

急成長中の枝豆人気

　豆腐と並んでアメリカで急速に一般的になりつつあるのが枝豆。「トーフ」と同様「エダマメ」という商品名でスーパーに冷凍物が出回るようになりました。手軽で健康的、ベジタリアンにもOKなおつまみとして人気です。枝豆は日本人の子供にも好かれますが、アメリカ人の子供にも比較的抵抗なく受け入れられます。

　日本料理店のメニューにも必ずあるのですが、その食べ方はさまざま。日本人のように慣れた手つきで豆を口に入れる人も中にはいますが、サヤを手であけて豆をつ

3. Dress the boiled green beans with the sesame dressing mixture (A). It does not matter if the beans have not fully cooled down, but be sure to dress just before serving.

* If you are overseas or just have trouble finding ground sesame seeds, you can make them yourself from raw sesame seeds. Distribute the seeds evenly on a baking sheet; try to expose all the seeds. Bake them at 180 C (350 F) until light brown (about 2 to 3 minutes). Grind the fragrant seeds finely using a mortar and pestle or a food processor. If using a food processor, be careful not to process too long; you do not want the oil to come out of the seeds.

Edamame—they are taking the United States by storm

Boiled green soybeans in their pods, *edamame*, are fast becoming a favorite with Americans right along with tofu. Just as "tofu" has become a trade name, *edamame* can be found in the frozen foods section of supermarkets labeled as "*edamame*." They are easy to prepare, healthy, and a fine appetizer for vegetarians. Japanese kids love them, and even kids in the United States do not resist them as much as they do some foods.

Edamame are on the menu at every Japanese restaurant, but the way they are eaten varies. While some Americans will pop the soybeans easily into

まみ出す人もよく見かけます。何も言われなければサヤごと食べてしまう豪傑もいます。指でサヤから押し出しながら豆だけを口に入れるのは、慣れないと意外に難しいものらしいのです。

冷凍枝豆は、手がまったくかからなくて安価な割には、立派な前菜の1品になるので、アメリカ人を招いたときにはとても便利です。ただし、枝豆を食べたことのないお客様がいるときには食べ方の説明を忘れずに。

焼き野菜料理

野菜を焼くと、野菜の香りや味が強く引き出されます。夏にバーベキューをする際には、ぜひ焼き野菜も加えてください。

焼きなす

なすの最もシンプルな食べ方のひとつです。温かくても冷たく冷やしても。

なす………4本
醤油

their mouths like we Japanese who are familiar with them do, you will also see many of them opening the pod with their fingers and picking out the individual soybeans. Then there are the real heroes out there who, not knowing any better, chew up the pod along with the soybeans. It is surprising how difficult it can be for some inexperienced people to gently squeeze the soybean out of its pod right into their mouths.

Frozen *edamame* are inexpensive and require little preparation, yet they make an outstanding appetizer, so they are convenient to have around if you are entertaining Americans. But, if there are any inexperienced guests, please do not forget to explain to them how *edamame* should be eaten.

Grilled vegetables

Grilling vegetables brings out their full flavor and aroma. Include some grilled vegetables on the menu at your next summer barbeque.

Grilled eggplant

This is one of the simplest ways of preparing eggplant. They can be served warm or chilled.

4 eggplants
Soy sauce

かつお節またはすりごま

1. なすは洗ってへたをとり、グリルなどでまるごと焼く。
2. 黒く焦げて中身がやわらかくなり、皮が割れて汁が吹き出すようになったら火からおろす。
3. 水をかけて冷やしながら、皮をむく。
4. 適当な大きさに割いて醤油をかけ、かつお節またはすりごまをかける。温かいうちもおいしいが、醤油を出汁(だし)で割ったものにつけて冷やすと夏らしい一品に。これもおひたしと同様に薄めためんつゆをかけてもいけます。

＊米なすとも呼ばれるアメリカのなすは赤ん坊の頭ほどもある巨大なもの。まるごと焼いて火を通すのはとても無理です。焼きなすにはイタリアン・エッグプラントとして売られているなすや、細長い中国なすを使ってください。

きのこホイル焼き

きのこはアメリカでも最近さまざまなものが出回るようになってきましたが、きのこそのものを味わう料理はまだ少ないように思えます。ポーティベロや大型のしいたけなどは直接グリルで焼いてもいいのですが、小さなきのこはホイルで包むのが最も簡単です。バターはオリーブオイルに代えてもかまいません。

Bonito flakes or ground sesame seeds

1. Wash eggplant and remove stem; grill whole on a grill plate, barbeque, etc.
2. Remove from the grill when the outside is nicely blackened, the inside is soft, and liquid can be seen coming out through the cracks in the skin.
3. Peel off skin while cooling under running water.
4. Cut into easy-to-eat pieces; top with a dash of soy sauce and bonito flakes or ground sesame seeds. Serve while still warm; alternatively, you can dilute soy sauce with *dashi*, add to eggplant, and chill for a cool summertime dish. As with *ohitashi*, you could pour thinned noodle broth over the eggplant.

* Eggplants common in the United States, which we refer to as "American eggplants," can be as big as a baby's head, so it is impossible to grill them whole. Use what are sold as "Italian eggplants" or the long, thin Chinese variety.

Mushrooms grilled in foil

A wide variety of mushrooms have become available recently in the United States, but it does not appear to me that they are enjoyed very often on their own. Big portobello and *shiitake* mushrooms can be grilled whole, but the easiest way to grill smaller mushrooms is by wrapping them in aluminum foil first. You can use olive oil instead of butter.

きのこ……適宜（しいたけ、えのきだけ、エリンギ、しめじなど）
醤油(しょうゆ)
酒
バター

1. きのこは汚れを落とし、食べやすい大きさに切っておく。
2. アルミホイルに切ったきのこをのせ、醤油と酒をかけ、バターひとかけらをのせてアルミホイルを閉じる。
3. ホイルごと焼く（オーブン、オーブントースター、グリルのいずれでも）。

根菜のオーブン焼き

　伝統的な日本の調理法ではありませんが、れんこんやごぼうなど、日本の根菜本来の味が最もよく引き出される調理方法だと思います。切り方は好みですが、拍子木切りが火の通りもよく、野菜の歯ごたえが楽しめます。

れんこん、ごぼう、にんじん、大根、いもなどの根菜類なら何でも
オリーブオイル
塩

1. 野菜は洗ってひと口大に切り（切り方は好みの形で）水気をふいておく。
2. 野菜にオリーブオイルと少量の塩をまぶし、グラタ

Mushrooms (*shiitake, enoki, eryngii, shimeji*, etc.), as needed.
Soy sauce
Sake
Butter

1. Clean any dirt off mushrooms; cut into bite-size pieces.
2. Place cut mushrooms on a sheet of aluminum foil; pour soy sauce and sake over them, add a pat of butter, seal foil.
3. Grill or bake.

Baked root vegetables

While this may not be a traditional form of Japanese cooking, it really brings out the flavor of Japanese root vegetables such as lotus and burdock root. You can cut the root vegetables any way you like, but cutting them into long sticks makes it easier for them to cook through thoroughly and retains some firmness.

Any root vegetables, such as lotus root, burdock root, carrots, *daikon*, and potatoes.
Olive oil
Salt

1. Wash vegetables and cut into bite-size pieces (you can cut them any way you like); pat dry.
2. Drizzle with olive oil and sprinkle with salt.

ン皿など、オーブンに入れられる皿に並べる。このときなるべく重ならないように大きめの皿を使った方がカリッと仕上がる。ない場合には天板に直接並べてもよい。

3 高温（摂氏220度・華氏425度くらい）のオーブンで、わずかに焦げ目がつくくらいまで焼く（5〜10分程度）。すぐに焼けるので、焦げないように様子をこまめにチェックすることが必要。

炒めて煮る

油を使うことで野菜の淡白な味にこくが加わります。きんぴらは、ほかにもれんこんやじゃがいも、大根などさまざまな根菜で同様につくれます。コツは最初によく炒めること。調味料を加えたあとも、さらに水気がなくなるまでよく炒めることで味が凝縮されます。

きんぴらごぼう

日本の家庭料理の定番です。濃い目の味つけがごはんにぴったり。

ごぼう	1本
にんじん	1本
醤油	大さじ2
みりん	大さじ2

Assemble in an oven-proof baking dish. Use a dish that is large enough that the vegetables are not piled on top of each other (They will come out crispier this way.) If you do not have a suitable baking dish, you can spread the vegetables out on a baking sheet.
3. Bake in a hot oven (about 220 C, or 425 F) until vegetables are just beginning to brown (about 5 to 10 minutes). They cook quickly, so keep a watch on them or they will burn.

Kinpira (saute and simmer) technique

Sauteing in oil brings body to otherwise bland vegetables. You can make *kinpira* in the same way with other root vegetables, such as lotus root, potatoes, and *daikon*. The trick is to first saute well. The taste will continue to concentrate while the liquid evaporates after you add the seasonings, so keep on sauteing.

Sauteed and simmered burdock root

This is a standard item in a Japanese home. The strong, rich taste goes great with rice.

1 burdock root
1 carrot
2 tablespoons soy sauce
2 tablespoons *mirin*

赤唐辛子（鷹の爪）……少々
ごま油………………………大さじ1

1. ごぼうは皮を包丁の背でこそげとり、斜め薄切りにしてから千切りにし、水につけてアクを抜く。

2. にんじんも斜め薄切りにしてから千切り。

3. 鍋にごま油と唐辛子を入れて熱し、水を切ったごぼうを中火で炒める。

4. ごぼうがしんなりしてきたらにんじんを加え、さらに炒める。

5. 1〜2分炒めたら、みりん、醤油を加え、水気がなくなるまで炒める。

＊ごぼうの皮は薄いので、普通は包丁の背でこそげとるようにむきますが、うまくできない場合には、丸めたアルミホイルでこすりながら水で流すときれいにむけます。

① 包丁の背で皮をこそげとる

② 斜め切りにしてから千切りにし、水につけてアクを抜く

Pinch of slivered red chili peppers (*takanotsume*)
1 tablespoon sesame oil

1. Rub the skin of the burdock root off with the blunt side of a knife. Slice thinly on the diagonal, then julienne the slices; soak in water to remove impurities.
2. Slice carrot on the diagonal; julienne.
3. Heat sesame oil and chili peppers in a saucepan. Drain the burdock root; add to saucepan and saute on medium heat.
4. When the burdock root softens, add carrot; continue sauteing.
5. Saute for another 1 to 2 minutes; add *mirin* and soy sauce. Simmer until liquid evaporates.

* The skin of burdock root is thin, so it is usually easiest to remove it by scraping with the blunt side of a knife. However, if you have trouble, you can remove it by rubbing it under running water with a scrunched up sheet of aluminum.

1. Remove the skin with the blunt edge of a knife.
2. Slice diagonally, julienne, and soak in water to remove astringency.

セロリきんぴら

日本ではセロリのきんぴらは一般的ではありませんが、香りがあっていいものです。繊維がしっかりしているので、長時間炒めてもしゃきしゃきした歯ざわりは損なわれません。斜め薄切りにするのでスジも気になりません。水分が多い野菜なので、水っぽさをとばすよう強火で炒めてください。

セロリ………… 1株
醤油(しょうゆ)………… 大さじ1
みりん………… 大さじ1
サラダ油…… 大さじ1
かつお節…… (削り節小1袋3g程度)

1. セロリは斜め薄切りにする。
2. 鍋に油を熱し、セロリを強火で炒める。
3. セロリがしんなりして水気がなくなってきたら、みりんと醤油を加えてさらに炒める。
4. 水気がなくなるまで炒めたら火からおろしてかつお節をまぶす。

ピーマンきんぴら

ピーマンは時間をかけてじっくり炒めると甘味が出てきます。特にアメリカ風の肉厚のものは驚くほど甘くなるので、味つけは醤油(しょうゆ)だけで十分です。

Sauteed and simmered celery

Celery *kinpira* is not common in Japan, but with its wonderful aroma, it works well. Since it is quite fibrous, it can be sauteed and simmered for a long time, and it will not lose much of its crispy, firm texture. If you slice the celery on the diagonal, you do not need to be concerned about it being stringy. Saute on high, because celery contains a lot of water which needs to be boiled off.

1 rib celery
1 tablespoon soy sauce
1 tablespoon *mirin*
1 tablespoon vegetable oil
Bonito flakes (1 small packet, about 3 g)

1. Slice celery thinly on the diagonal.
2. Heat oil in saucepan; saute celery on high heat.
3. When the celery has softened and lost much of its moisture, add the soy sauce and *mirin*; simmer.
4. Remove from heat when liquid is gone; sprinkle with bonito flakes.

Sauteed and simmered green peppers

Green peppers become sweet when sauteed for long periods of time. This is especially true with the thick-walled green bell peppers you find in the United States. They become really, really sweet, so they only need to be seasoned with soy sauce.

ピーマン‥‥アメリカサイズなら1個、
　　　　　　日本のものなら4〜6個
ごま油‥‥‥‥小さじ2
醤油‥‥‥‥‥大さじ1
かつお節‥‥（削り節小1袋3g程度）またはすりごま（小さじ
　　　　　　2程度）

1. ピーマンは繊維に沿って、縦に細切りにする。
2. 鍋にごま油を熱し、ピーマンを中火でよく炒める。
3. ピーマンがしんなりして水気が少なくなってきたら醤油を加え、さらによく炒める。
4. 水気がなくなるまで炒めたら火からおろし、かつお節またはすりごまをまぶす。

揚げ野菜

世界中で愛されているフライドポテトをはじめ、揚げた野菜は子供にも人気のあるもの。野菜、特に根菜類は揚げると甘味が引き出され、塩をふっただけでもおいしく食べられます。

精進揚げ

天ぷらは寿司に先がけて海外に紹介された日本料理ですが、精進揚げのおいしさは今ひとつ知られていないと思います。日本料理店では「ベジタブル・テンプラ」と

- 1 green bell pepper (or 4 to 6 Japanese green peppers)
- 2 teaspoons sesame oil
- 1 tablespoon soy sauce
- 1 small packet bonito flakes, about 3 g, or 2 teaspoons ground sesame seeds

1. Slice green peppers lengthwise, along the grain, in thin strips.
2. Heat oil in saucepan; saute on medium heat.
3. When the green peppers soften and lose much of their moisture, add soy sauce; simmer.
4. Continue simmering until liquid evaporates; remove from heat. Sprinkle with bonito flakes or ground sesame seeds.

Deep-fried vegetables

Kids around the world love deep-fried vegetables, such as French fries. Deep-frying brings out the sweetness of vegetables, especially root vegetables, and then all they need is a little salt.

Vegetable tempura

Tempura was introduced overseas before sushi, but I do not think the wonderful taste of vegetable tempura is fully appreciated. "Vegetable Tempura" is on the menu

してメニューに載っていますが、食べてみると素材のチョイスひとつとっても首をかしげるものばかりです。切り方も必ずしも素材に合っていません。

　精進揚げは天つゆで食べてもいいのですが、塩または生醬油で食べたほうが野菜の味が生きるように思います。また、そうめんなどの冷たい麺類との相性は抜群です。

にんじん……1本
ごぼう………½本
いんげん……200g
天ぷら粉
揚げ油

1. にんじんは皮をむいて斜め薄切りにしてから、太めのマッチ棒くらいに千切りにする。
2. ごぼうは皮をこそげおとしてから2ミリ程度の斜め薄切りにして、水にさらす。
3. いんげんはスジをとっておく。
4. ボウルに天ぷら粉を入れ、パッケージの指示どおりの水で溶いて衣をつくる。
5. 野菜は水気を切り、天ぷら粉または小麦粉をまぶしておく。
6. 小さなボウルににんじんを少し入れ、大さじ1程度の天ぷらの衣をつけてまとめ、熱した揚げ油に入れて揚げる。
7. ごぼうは1枚ずつ、衣をできるだけ薄くつけて揚げる。
8. いんげんはにんじん同様に、数本ずつ衣でまとめて

at every Japanese restaurant, but the vegetables they use for it are questionable. I also think that the way they cut them is sometimes wrong, not suiting that particular vegetable.

You can eat vegetable tempura with tempura sauce, but I prefer a little salt or a dash of pure soy sauce as this lets you enjoy the real flavor of the vegetables. It is also an outstanding match for *somen* and other cold noodles.

1 carrot
½ burdock root
200 g green beans
Tempura flour
Oil for frying

1. Peel carrots and slice thinly on the diagonal; julienne the slices into somewhat large matchstick-size strips.
2. Scrape off burdock root skin. Cut on the diagonal in 2 mm thick slices; immerse in water.
3. Trim green beans.
4. Put tempura flour and water (according to package instructions) in a bowl; mix to form a batter.
5. Dry vegetables; coat with tempura flour or ordinary flour.
6. Place carrots in a small bowl. Add about 1 tablespoon of tempura batter; combine and fry in hot oil.
7. Lightly coat the burdock root slices with tempura batter; fry one at a time.
8. Coat several green beans at a time in tempura

揚げる。

*天ぷら粉がない場合には、小麦粉¾カップと片栗粉½カップをよくまぜておいてから炭酸水1カップで溶いて衣にします。普通の天ぷらの衣（小麦粉と卵と水）より、失敗なくカラッと揚がります。

れんこん肉詰め

れんこんは、数ある日本野菜の中でも、最もアメリカ人受けのいいものの1つです。形の面白さもありますが、カリカリとしながらモチモチしたところもある独特の歯ごたえは、子供にも人気があります。この肉詰めは揚げてもいいのですが、少量の油で炒め揚げのようにしたほうが、失敗なくできます。味つけはしていないので、食卓で塩または醬油をつけながら召し上がってください。

れんこん…………2本
牛赤身ひき肉…200g
小麦粉……………1カップ
油…………………適量

1 れんこんは皮をむき、5ミリ厚さの輪切りにする。
2 れんこんの輪切りの両面に小麦粉をまぶし、ひき肉大さじ1杯分くらいを片面に塗りつける。同様に小麦粉を両面にまぶした別の輪切りれんこん1枚をその上に重ね、肉をギュッとはさむ。このときれんこ

batter, as with the carrots; fry together in batches.

* If you do not have tempura flour, combine ¾ cup flour and ½ cup cornstarch; mix well. Stir in 1 cup of soda water and mix to form a batter. You will have better, crispier results using this batter than ordinary tempura batter (flour, eggs and water).

Lotus root stuffed with meat

Of the many Japanese vegetables used in Japanese cooking, lotus root is one of the most popular with Americans. The shape is interesting, and while being crunchy they have a springy texture, making them popular even among kids. Here we are frying the lotus root stuffed with meat, but you will have better results using only a small amount of oil. It is not seasoned while cooking, so salt or sprinkle with soy sauce at the table.

2 lotus roots
200 g lean ground beef
1 cup flour
Oil for frying

1. Remove lotus root skin; slice in 5 mm rounds.
2. Coat both sides of 1 round with flour; spread about 1 tablespoon of ground beef on top of one side. Coat a second round with flour; put it on top of the ground beef, forming a sandwich. Now, the trick is

んの穴にひき肉が入るくらいしっかりはさんでおくのがコツ。

③ さらに肉詰めれんこん1つひとつに小麦粉をよくまぶす。

④ フライパンにサラダ油を5ミリくらい入れて熱し、肉をはさんだれんこんの両面を、中火で火が通るまで焼く（片面2分程度）。焼き上がったらペーパータオルなどで油を切る。

to press them firmly together so that the meat fills the lotus root's holes.
3. Coat the stuffed lotus root again with plenty of flour.
4. Fill a frying pan with about 5 mm of vegetable oil; heat. Fry both sides of the stuffed lotus root on medium heat until cooked through (about 2 minutes per side). Drain on paper towel.

5

豆腐には味がある
Tofu—It Has Taste

日本伝統の健康食

　日本の伝統食材の中でも、特に世界的に脚光を浴びているのが豆腐です。植物系のたんぱく源として優れているだけでなく、体にいいイソフラボンが含まれています。こうした健康上のメリットが注目されるようになり、豆腐はアメリカのスーパーでも簡単に手に入るようになりました。

　日本国内でも、健康志向からさまざまな高級豆腐ブランドが出現し、自家製豆腐を看板メニューにする居酒屋も増えています。おいしい豆腐なら、そのまま冷奴や湯豆腐で食べるのが一番ですが、まだまだ外国では手に入る豆腐の質には限りがあります。また、豆腐の淡白なおいしさは、ある程度食べ慣れないとなかなかわかりにくいものなので、外国人に出す場合は、始めはしっかりした味つけの豆腐料理のほうが受け入れてもらえると思います。

ヘルシーだけど味がない、という誤解

　豆腐がヘルシーな食材だということは、今やアメリカでも常識。ある程度健康を意識している人ならば、豆腐を買って食べたことが一度や二度はあるはずです。でも、日常的に食生活にとり入れている人は多くありませ

Japan's traditional health food

Of the many healthy traditional Japanese foods, tofu in particular has held center stage throughout the world. This is not only because tofu is a fantastic source of protein, but because it also contains isoflavones. After these health-related factors became the focus of attention, tofu became easily available on the shelves of supermarkets all over the United States.

With the growing health consciousness in Japan, many high-end brands of tofu appeared; more and more Japanese-style pubs are even advertising homemade tofu. A tasty tofu is best served chilled with some toppings, but outside of Japan the quality of the tofu is on the low side. The plain yet delicious taste of tofu takes some getting used to before it can be fully appreciated, so if you are going to serve it to foreigners, I suggest you use flavorful recipes first.

It is healthy, but tasteless —the misconception

It is common knowledge, even in the United States these days, that tofu is good for you. Anyone who is even mildly concerned about their health has bought and eaten a package or two of it. However, not many

ん。理由は「味がない」から。何カ月もスーパーの棚に並んでいる真空パックの豆腐をそのまま食べても「味がない」のは当然です。サラダのトッピングとして小さく切った豆腐がサラダバーに並んでいたりしますが、いかにもまずそう。豆腐は知っていてもそのおいしい食べ方はまだまだ知られていないのです。豆腐を使ったレシピがあちこちに出回ってはいますが、豆腐の味を消してしまうスムージーやチョコレートケーキなどでは、豆腐本来の味はますますわかりません。

豆腐がどこでも買えるようになっただけに、かえってアメリカ人の多くは「トーフはヘルシーだけど味がない」という先入観を持ってしまっています。ですから、マーボー豆腐など濃い味つけで「豆腐っておいしいかも」と思える料理はとても喜ばれます。

豆腐そのものを味わう料理

本当においしい豆腐は塩をつけ食べてもおいしいものですが、それは上質の豆腐が手に入るという条件があってのこと。そこそこの豆腐をおいしく食べるには、タレに工夫が必要です。

冷奴

上等な豆腐ならお塩か醤油だけで、今ひとつな豆腐は

Americans include it in their diets on a daily basis. The reason, they claim, is that it is tasteless. Well, it goes without saying that a vacuum packed lump of tofu that has been on a supermarket's shelf for months is tasteless if it is just opened and eaten as is. You see small cubes of tofu on display at salad bars, meant to be a topping, and they look terrible. Americans may know about tofu, but they sure do not know how to make tasty dishes with it. Recipes using tofu abound, but if you make a smoothie out of it or chocolate cake, not even a hint of tofu's taste remains, so it is even harder to appreciate it.

It seems that the more readily available tofu has become in the United States, the greater the preconception that it is a healthy but tasteless food. For that reason, they use it for rich-tasting dishes such as Chinese mapo tofu and get excited, thinking, "Wow, tofu might just be tasty after all."

Recipes for enjoying the taste of tofu

Truly tasty tofu can be enjoyed as is with a sprinkle of salt, but that is assuming such high quality tofu can be found. For average tofu, a good sauce is essential.

Chilled tofu with toppings

High-quality tofu needs only a sprinkle of salt or a dash

5 豆腐には味がある

ちょっと濃厚な味のタレでどうぞ。

絹ごし豆腐............ 1丁
ねぎダレ（A）
　わけぎ............ 1本
　かつお節............ 5g
　醤油............ 大さじ2
　オリーブ油......... 大さじ1
　バルサミコ酢...... 大さじ1
ごまダレ（B）
　すりごま............ 大さじ2
　めんつゆ............ 大さじ2

1 豆腐は8つくらいに切ってよく冷やしておく。
2 それぞれのタレの材料を合わせる。
3 冷やした豆腐の水を切って好みのタレをかける。

湯豆腐

コツは煮すぎないこと。熱々が一番の料理ではありますが、煮すぎると豆腐の風味と甘味ががっくりと落ちます。水から火にかけてグラグラっと沸いてきたくらいで火を止めます。

豆腐（木綿、絹ごしのいずれでも）.... 1丁
昆布............ 10センチ角程度
醤油ダレ（A）
　醤油.......... 大さじ2

of soy sauce, but inferior tofu needs a rich sauce.

1 block *kinu* (soft) tofu
Scallion sauce (A)
    1 scallion
    5 g bonito flakes
    2 tablespoons soy sauce
    1 tablespoon olive oil
    1 tablespoon balsamic vinegar
Sesame sauce (B)
    2 tablespoons ground sesame
    2 tablespoons noodle broth

1. Cut tofu block into about 8 cubes; chill well.
2. Mix both sauces.
3. Drain chilled tofu; pour sauce of your liking over tofu.

Simmered tofu

The trick to this dish is not simmering the tofu for too long. This dish is best served piping hot, but if you simmer it for too long the tofu will lose its flavor and sweetness. Begin with the tofu in water and gradually bring to a boil; turn off heat.

1 block tofu (soft or firm)
10-cm square piece of *konbu*
Soy sauce-based sauce (A)
    2 tablespoons soy sauce

出汁………… 大さじ2
かつお節…… 5g

1. (A)の材料を合わせてタレをつくる。
2. 豆腐は8つくらいに切り、たっぷりの水を張った厚手の鍋に昆布と一緒に入れる。
3. 鍋を強火にかけ、沸騰し始めたら火を止める。
4. 鍋ごと食卓に運び、各自が豆腐を器にとってタレをかける。

＊冷奴（ひややっこ）に使うねぎダレやごまダレも合います。

田楽

　本来は焼き網を使って焼くものですが、オーブントースターやフライパンでも手軽につくれます。串に差したものはパーティー受けするので、おもてなしにはぜひ串刺しスタイルで。お豆腐は硬めのものを選んでください。

木綿豆腐または焼き豆腐… 1丁
オリーブオイル……………… 大さじ1
練り味噌（みそ）…………………………（味噌100g、酒大さじ3、みりん大さじ2、砂糖大さじ3）

1. 豆腐はよく水切りをしておく。
2. 鍋に練り味噌の材料を入れてまぜ、弱火で練りながら火を通す。
3. 水切りした豆腐を半分に切ってから、さらに半分の厚さに切り、それぞれをさらに3つに切る（12個の

2 tablespoons *dashi*
  5 g bonito flakes

1. Combine sauce ingredients.
2. Cut tofu into about 8 cubes. Place in a heavy saucepan with plenty of water; add *konbu*.
3. Heat on high until just boiling; turn off heat.
4. Bring saucepan to the table; allow diners to serve the tofu and sauce themselves.

* The scallion sauce and sesame sauce used for chilled tofu also work well with simmered tofu.

Dengaku (tofu coated in a *miso* sauce and grilled)

These were traditionally grilled, but they can easily be made in a toaster oven or even cooked in a frying pan. Skewered *dengaku* are popular at parties, so they are the type to prepare in such cases. Use firm tofu.

  1 block regular (firm) tofu or grilled tofu
  1 tablespoon olive oil
  Prepared *miso* (100 g *miso*, 3 tablespoons sake, 2 tablespoons *mirin*, and 3 tablespoons sugar)

1. Thoroughly dry tofu.
2. Prepare the *miso* ingredients in a saucepan on low heat; cook thoroughly.
3. Cut dried tofu in half, then cut each half to half its thickness; cut these in thirds, making a total of 12

長方形になる)。

4 それぞれの豆腐の両面にオリーブオイルを塗る。

5 テフロン加工のフライパンに重ならないように並べ、ところどころきつね色になるまで中火で焼く。このとき途中で豆腐を動かさないことがポイント。片面が焼けたら裏返す。

6 両面がこんがり焼けたら、アルミホイルかオーブンシートを敷いた天板に並べ、片面（上）に練り味噌を塗る。

7 オーブントースターで味噌が少しこんがりするまで焼く。焦げやすいので注意する。

8 串に刺す場合は、豆腐の長いほうに沿って1本ずつ刺す。

*豆腐の水切り

豆腐は水分を多く含んでいるので、調理の前に水切りが必要です（冷奴のように豆腐の水分によるやわらかさを味わう場合には必要ありません）。特に田楽のように形をくずしたくない場合にはしっかり水切りすることが大切です。水切りの方法は3つあります。

①重しをする

ペーパータオルに包んでその上にお皿などを置いて重しとし、30分〜1時間以上置きます。時間はかかりますが、一番失敗のない方法で、形もくずれません。

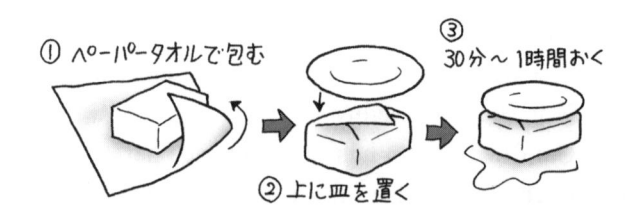

① ペーパータオルで包む
② 上に皿を置く
③ 30分〜1時間おく

rectangular pieces.

4. Coat both sides of the tofu pieces with olive oil.
5. Arrange in a Teflon-coated frying pan, ensuring that they do not overlap; cook on medium heat until lightly browned. The trick here is to make sure you do not move them around as they brown. When one side is finished browning, turn over.
6. When both sides are nicely browned, assemble them on a baking sheet covered with aluminum foil or parchment paper; coat top sides with prepared *miso*.
7. Bake in a toaster oven until golden brown. They burn easily, so be careful.
8. If you are going to skewer them, do it in the long direction.

* How to dry tofu

Tofu contains a lot of water, so for some dishes it is important to dry it before cooking with it (tofu for dishes that are meant to be soft, such as chilled tofu with toppings, does not need to be dried). This is especially true for *dengaku* as you do not want it to crumble. For this kind of a dish, you really must remove as much water as you can. There are three ways to do this.

1. Pressing

   Wrap tofu in paper towel and set a plate or some other item on top as a weight for 30 minutes to 1 hour. It takes a bit of time, but this is the best way to remove the water; the tofu retains its shape well, too.

---

1. Wrap in a paper towel.
2. Put a plate on top.
3. Let sit for 30 minutes to 1 hour.

②ゆでる

5分ほどゆでることで水気が抜けて固くなります。田楽のように過熱する料理に向きます。

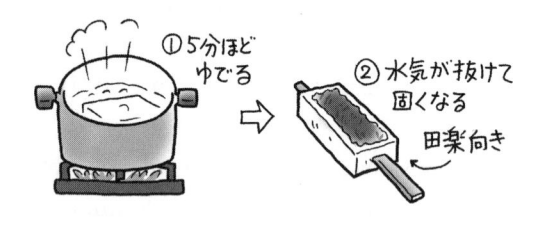

③電子レンジにかける

ペーパータオルに包んで1～2分加熱します。一番早くできますが、加熱しすぎると味を損なうので注意が必要です。豆腐によって水分の含有量も異なるので様子を見ながら加熱してください。

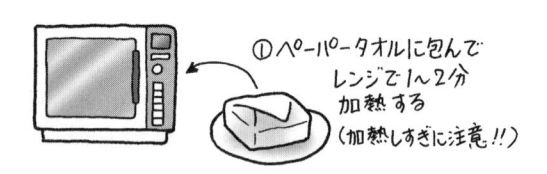

練り味噌バリエーション

練り味噌は豆腐田楽のほか、ゆでた野菜などさまざまなものに添えて楽しめます。また、使う味噌によって甘味辛味も違ってきますので、いろいろ試してみてください。上記の基本の練り味噌にさまざまな材料を加えればバリエーションも広がります。

2. Boiling

Five minutes of boiling will remove excess water and make the tofu firm. For a dish that will be heated, such as *dengaku*, this is a good method.

---

1. Boil for 5 minutes.
2. Tofu will release water and become firm (good for *dengaku*).

3. Microwave

Wrap in paper towel; heat in a microwave oven for 1 to 2 minutes. This is the fastest method, but if you heat it too much it will lose its flavor, so be careful. The moisture content of tofu differs from one tofu to another, so watch it while you heat it.

---

1. Wrap in a paper towel and heat in a microwave oven for 1 or 2 minutes (do not overheat).

Prepared *miso*—variations

In addition to *dengaku*, prepared *miso* is a great accompaniment to boiled vegetables and all sorts of other foods. And, since some types of *miso* are sweet while others are salty, try all the variations you can think of. The above recipe is a base to work with; you can add all sorts of ingredients.

- ねぎ味噌（刻んだねぎ1本分を加えて弱火で練る）

- ごま味噌（すりごま大さじ1杯を加えて弱火で練る）

- 鶏味噌（鶏ひき肉50gを炒めてから練り味噌を加えて練る）

5 油揚げの素焼き

豆腐に比べ油揚げはまだまったくといっていいほどアメリカでは知られていません。焼いてパリっとさせた油揚げは簡単でおいしい前菜になります。

油揚げ……2枚
わけぎ……1本（小口切り）
醤油

1. 鍋に熱湯をわかし、油揚げをくぐらせて油抜きをする。
2. 油揚げの水気をよくしぼってからオーブントースターまたはグリルでこんがりと焼く。
3. 両面焼いて油揚げがパリッとなったら熱いうちにわけぎをのせ、醤油をかける。

＊わけぎの代わりにしょうが醤油や大根おろし醤油もおすすめします。

- Scallions *miso* (add a finely chopped scallions and cook on low heat)
- Sesame *miso* (add 1 tablespoon ground sesame and cook on low heat)
- Chicken *miso* (saute 50 g minced chicken; add *miso* mixture and cook)

Grilled *aburaage* (regular tofu that has been cut in thin slices and deep fried)

Compared with tofu, it would not be an exaggeration to say that *aburaage* is completely unknown in the United States. Grilled or broiled until crisp, it is simple to prepare and makes delicious a appetizer.

2 sheets *aburaage*
1 stalk scallions (chopped finely)
Soy sauce

1. Bring water to a boil in a saucepan; dip *aburaage* in boiling water to remove oil.
2. Squeeze out excess water; grill or broil in a toaster oven until it is golden brown.
3. When both sides are golden brown and crisp, remove and serve hot, sprinkled with scallions and a dash of soy sauce.

* An alternative to scallions is using a ginger/soy sauce mix or a grated daikon/soy sauce mix.

最近はやりのグルメ系豆腐は
初心者にもわかる濃厚な旨味(うまみ)

　最近日本では、ちょっと高いグルメ豆腐のブランドが次々と登場しています。いずれもこれまでの豆腐より濃厚な旨味があります。鮮度が大切なのでなかなか海外では手に入りませんが、たまに日本食料品店に並ぶことがあります。こうしたグルメ豆腐をほんの少しずつ器に入れて、上質の塩をかけて出すと外国人にも「フロマージュブランのようだ」と喜ばれます。もともと高い豆腐を日本から運んでいるのですから、豆腐とは思えないような値段ですが、チーズだと思えば納得できる価格です。新しい味を試すのが好きなお客様には手軽に喜んでもらえる一品です。

しっかり味つけした豆腐料理

　肉やスパイスで味を補った豆腐料理は、豆腐嫌いの人にも喜ばれます。ベジタリアンには向かないのが玉にキズですが、お肉大好きの男性や子供にも好評です。

Gourmet tofu—gaining in popularity, even beginners can appreciate its rich taste

In Japan, somewhat expensive gourmet tofu brands are continuing to grow in number on store shelves. They all are much richer in taste than ordinary tofu. Because freshness is so important, these types of tofu are very difficult to get overseas, but you can occasionally find them at a Japanese food specialty store. Served in very small portions with a sprinkling of top-quality salt, even foreigners will be overjoyed, claiming it tastes like *fromage blanc*. Since this tofu is expensive to begin with and has to be transported from Japan, it has a surprising price tag, but it is not that bad if you think of it as a good cheese. You can easily bring joy to your favorite guests by letting them taste something entirely new to them.

Full-flavored tofu dishes

Tofu dishes supplemented with meats and spices are enjoyed by even those people who do not like tofu. These dishes are not suited to vegetarians, their only weakness, but they are very popular with meat-eating men and kids.

肉豆腐

濃い目の味つけで肉の味がしみるまでじっくり煮込みます。ごはんにかけて牛丼風にしてもよいでしょう。

木綿豆腐…………1丁
牛肉または豚肉の薄切り……200g
たまねぎ…………小1個
醤油…………大さじ4
砂糖…………大さじ2
サラダ油…………大さじ1
出汁または水……2カップ

1. 豆腐は8つくらいに切る。
2. たまねぎは薄切りにする。
3. 鍋にサラダ油を熱し、強火でたまねぎを炒める。
4. たまねぎがしんなりしてきたら肉を入れ、さらに火が通るまで炒める。
5. 肉にも火が通ったら、調味料を入れて煮立てる。
6. 豆腐を入れて、出汁または水を加えて、豆腐に火が通るまで煮込む。

マーボー豆腐

正確には日本料理ではなく中華料理ですが、カレーやラーメンと同じく日本のお総菜の1つと考えてもいいと思います。私がつくる豆腐料理の中でアメリカ人にダントツの人気なのがマーボー豆腐です。これもごはんにか

Braised meat and tofu

This is best if simmered for a long time to let the richly-seasoned meat flavor penetrate the tofu. It can also be served *donburi*-style on top of a big bowl of rice.

1 block regular (firm) tofu
200 g beef or pork, sliced thinly
1 small onion
4 tablespoons soy sauce
2 tablespoons sugar
1 tablespoon vegetable oil
2 cups *dashi* or water

1. Cut tofu in about 8 pieces.
2. Slice onion finely.
3. Heat oil in saucepan; saute onion on high heat.
4. Add meat when onion softens; continue sauteing until cooked through.
5. When meat is cooked through, add seasonings; simmer.
6. Add tofu and *dashi* (or water); continue to simmer until tofu is heated through.

Mapo tofu

This is actually not a Japanese dish, it is Chinese in origin, but like curry and ramen, it can be thought of as a standard dish in Japan. Of all the tofu dishes I prepare for Americans, mapo tofu is by far the most popular. I

けるマーボー丼スタイルもおすすめです。

木綿豆腐……………… 1丁
ひき肉（牛、豚、鶏のいずれでも）……100g
ねぎ………………… 日本ねぎなら1本、わけぎなら3本
にんにく…………… 2かけ
しょうが…………… 1かけ（2センチ角程度）
赤唐辛子…………… 少々
合わせ調味料（A）
　味噌（みそ）……………… 大さじ1
　醤油（しょうゆ）……………… 大さじ3
　みりん…………… 大さじ2
　酒………………… 大さじ1
　バルサミコ酢…… 小さじ1
　ごま油…………… 小さじ1
サラダ油…………… 大さじ1
片栗粉（かたくりこ）……………… 小さじ1（大さじ1程度の水で溶く）

1 にんにく、しょうが、ねぎはみじん切りにしておく。
2 豆腐は水切りをして、2センチ角くらいのさいの目に切る。
3 （A）の合わせ調味料の材料をまぜておく。
4 鍋にサラダ油と、にんにく、しょうが、唐辛子を入れて中火にかけ、油が熱くなってきたらねぎを加え、しんなりするまで炒める。

also recommend serving it *donburi*-style on top of a big bowl of rice.

- 1 block regular (firm) tofu
- 100 g ground meat (beef, pork, or chicken)
- 1 stalk Japanese leek (*negi*) or 3 stalks scallions (scallion)
- 2 cloves garlic
- 1 piece (about 2-cm) ginger
- 1 pinch red chili pepper
- Seasoning mix (A)
    - 1 tablespoon *miso*
    - 3 tablespoons soy sauce
    - 2 tablespoons *mirin*
    - 1 tablespoon sake
    - 1 teaspoon balsamic vinegar
    - 1 teaspoon sesame oil
- 1 tablespoon vegetable oil
- 1 teaspoon cornstarch (1 tablespoon powder mixed with water)

1. Finely chop garlic, ginger, and scallions.
2. Dry tofu thoroughly; cut into about 2-cm cubes.
3. Combine seasonings (A).
4. Pour vegetable oil into saucepan; heat garlic, ginger, and red chili pepper on medium. When the oil is hot, add the scallions; saute until soft.

5 肉を加え、完全に火が通るまで炒める。
6 合わせた調味料を入れ、さらに1分ほど炒めたら豆腐を入れる。
7 豆腐に火が通ったら（2〜3分）、水で溶いた片栗粉をいれ、すぐによくまぜて、とろみがつくまでさらに炒める（1分程度）。

ちょっと手のかかった豆腐料理

手はかかりますが、捨てがたい味わいの豆腐料理があります。必ずしも外国人受けするとは限りませんが、わかる人はとても喜んでくれます。特にベジタリアンのグルメにはおすすめです。

白和え

豆腐を和え衣にした和え物です。和え衣の味が主役ですから、たっぷりと用意します。和える素材は好き好きですが、しいたけなど味のついたもの、緑の野菜などを2、3種類組み合わせると彩りも味わいもよくなります。

木綿豆腐…………½丁
練りごま…………大さじ1
塩 ………………小さじ½
醤油………………小さじ½

5. Add meat and saute until completely cooked through.
6. Add seasoning mix. Continue sauteing for 1 minute; add tofu cubes.
7. When tofu is heated through (2 to 3 minutes), add mixed cornstarch; immediately stir well and continue sauteing until thickened (about 1 minute).

High-maintenance tofu

It takes some work, but there is one tofu dish that has to be included. It is not necessarily a foreigner-friendly dish, but those who know it, love it. This is especially the case with gourmet vegetarian types.

Shira-ae (mashed tofu salad)

Shira-ae is a salad-like mixture of vegetables dressed in a tofu coating. The tofu coating carries the flavor, so be sure to prepare plenty of it. What you dress depends on your likes and dislikes, but flavorful ingredients, such as *shiitake* mushrooms and green leafy vegetables of 2 or 3 types should be used for taste, as well as aesthetics.

½ block regular (firm) tofu
1 tablespoon sesame paste
½ teaspoon salt
½ teaspoon soy sauce

砂糖……………小さじ1
青菜類（水菜、ほうれん草、クレソンなど）……¼把
干ししいたけ…3枚
にんじん…………⅓本

1. 豆腐はペーパータオルに包んでお皿などを上に置いて重しにし、30分〜1時間おいてしっかり水切りしておく。
2. 干ししいたけは戻して細切りにし、醤油と砂糖各大さじ1を戻し汁に加え、煮て冷ましておく（＊まとめて戻して味つけしてから冷凍しておくと楽です。90ページ参照）。
3. 青菜はたっぷりのお湯に塩を入れてゆで、水にさらし、水気を絞ってから2〜3センチの長さに切る。
4. にんじんは斜めに薄切りしてから千切りにし、塩少々と酒大さじ1でしんなりするまで煮て冷ましておく。
5. 水切りした豆腐を（水切りに関しては184ページ）ペーパータオルまたは清潔な布巾に包んで、手でしぼってさらに水分を抜いてから茶漉しや目の細かいザルなどで裏ごし、調味料を加えてよくまぜる。
6. 食べる直前に材料を豆腐の和え衣で和える。

½ teaspoon sugar

¼ bunch green leafy vegetables (such as *mizuna*, spinach, watercress)

3 dried *shiitake* mushrooms

⅓ carrot

1. Press out the water from the tofu by wrapping it in paper towels and placing a plate or another object on top as a weight for 30 minutes to 1 hour.
2. Reconstitute dried mushrooms; slice thinly. Add 1 tablespoon each of soy sauce and sugar to mushroom liquid; simmer, then chill (For convenience, you can reconstitute the whole bag of mushrooms, season, and freeze [see page 91]).
3. Boil leafy vegetable in plenty of boiling salted water; rinse with water. After squeezing out excess water, slice in 2-to 3-cm lengths.
4. Slice carrot thinly on the diagonal; julienne. Simmer in 1 tablespoon sake and a pinch of salt.
5. Dry tofu (see page 185 for detailed instructions), and wrap the tofu with a paper towel or a kitchen cloth and squeez with your hands to remove more water. Pass through a tea strainer or fine strainer to puree; mix well with other seasonings.
6. Dress vegetables just before serving.

6

肉、魚、卵のおかず
Meat, Fish, and Eggs

魚は日本の健康食

　アメリカに住むと、いかに日本が魚に恵まれているかがわかります。アメリカではスーパーなどの魚売り場でも、種類も鮮度も本当に限られていて、常に手に入るのはサケやマグロ、カジキなどの切り身ばかり。これでは、魚はシンプルな塩焼きや刺身が一番などと言っていては食べられる魚がありません。

　ここでは品質が今ひとつでも、おいしく食べられる魚料理をご紹介します。ただし、シーフードに最低限の鮮度は欠かせません。アメリカのスーパーで売られている魚は大半が冷凍を解凍したものです。冷凍であることは問題ないのですが、少なくとも解凍したてのものを選んでください。その意味ではむしろ冷凍のものを購入してストックしておくほうが安心です。

　あまり脂ののっていない魚はオリーブオイルを使うとおいしくなります。

照り焼き

　醤油とみりんの甘辛ダレなら冷凍の切り身でもおいしく食べられます。夏場はバーベキューにすればさらに風味が増します。

Fish—Japan's health food

If you have lived in the United States, you know how lucky Japan is when it comes to the variety of fish available. Just go to the fish section of any supermarket in the United States—you will be amazed at the limited number of fish varieties and their lack of freshness. You can really only get portions of salmon, tuna, and swardfish. You might think that fish would be great simply salted and grilled or even as sashimi, but that is not the case.

Here are some recipes that work well even if the quality of the fish is not very good. But, do not overlook the fact that there is a limit to how low the quality of seafood can be that you can get away with using. The majority of fish being sold in the United States is originally frozen and then thawed out. There is nothing wrong with frozen fish, but you need to be careful to choose freshly thawed out products. In fact, you are better off buying frozen fish and storing it in your freezer.

Leaner fish can be made tastier using olive oil.

Teriyaki

The sweet/salty combination of *mirin* and soy sauce makes frozen cuts of fish quite tasty. Serving this at a summertime barbeque is especially appealing.

魚の切り身（カジキ、マグロ、ハマチ、サケなど）……4切れ
漬け汁（A）
　醤油…………大さじ3
　みりん………大さじ3　（＊みりんがない場合はみりん大さじ
　　　　　　　　　　　　1に対し砂糖大さじ½で代用します。）
　酒……………大さじ1
サラダ油………大さじ1

1. 漬け汁（A）の材料をすべて合わせて魚を1時間以上漬け込む。
2. グリルまたはオーブンで火が通るまで焼く。焦げやすいので火を強くしすぎないように注意する。

味噌漬け

　脂ののった魚に合う味です。にんにくやしょうがなどをすりおろして加えれば変化が楽しめます。

　また、買ってきた切り身をすぐに食べないときにも味噌漬けにしておくと3日目くらいまでおいしく食べられます。

魚切り身……4切れ
（カジキ、ハマチ、ギンダラ、チリアンシーバス、サケなど）
漬け味噌（A）
　味噌…………大さじ4
　みりん………大さじ2
　砂糖…………大さじ1
　酒……………大さじ1

4 fish fillets (swordfish, tuna, yellowtail, salmon, etc.)
Teriyaki marinade (A)
  3 tablespoons soy sauce
  3 tablespoons *mirin* (if you do not have *mirin*, substitute ½ tablespoon of sugar for each tablespoon of *mirin*)
  1 tablespoon sake
1 tablespoon vegetable oil

1. Marinate fish filets in marinade mix (A) for at least 1 hour.
2. Grill or broil in a oven heat until cooked through. Teriyaki burns easily, so be careful not to use too much heat.

Miso marinade

This is great with more oily types of fish. The flavor is further enhanced by the grated garlic and ginger.

And, if you cannot use the fish fillets immediately, they can be marinated in the *miso* combination for up to three days and still taste wonderful.

4 fish fillets (swordfish, yellowtail, sablefish, Chilean sea bass, salmon, etc.)
Miso marinade (A)
  4 tablespoons *miso*
  2 tablespoons *mirin*
  1 tablespoon sugar
  1 tablespoon sake

好みでしょうがや、にんにくのすりおろし……小さじ１

1. 漬け味噌(A)の材料をすべてよくまぜる。
2. 切り身にまぶしつけるようにして、ビニール袋などに密閉して冷蔵庫に入れてひと晩おく。
3. 焼く直前に味噌をペーパータオルなどでふきとる。
4. グリルまたはオーブントースターで火が通るまで焼く。

味噌焼き

漬け込む時間がいらず、すぐにつくれます。味噌はそのままでは味がきついのですが、マヨネーズを加えることでマイルドになります。この味噌ダレはごはんにもとてもよく合います。

切り身または半身の魚（骨なしなら何でも）……約400グラム
味噌ダレ（A）
　味噌……………大さじ２
　みりん…………大さじ２
　マヨネーズ……大さじ２
　醤油……………小さじ１
わけぎ……………３本
香菜………………みじん切り大さじ３

1. わけぎは薄い小口切りに、香菜も細かく切っておく。
2. 味噌ダレ(A)の材料をすべてまぜてからわけぎと香

1 teaspoon grated garlic or ginger, or to taste

1. Mix marinade ingredients.
2. Rub the marinade into the fish fillets; put in an airtight container or plastic bag and refrigerate overnight.
3. Just before grilling, remove *miso* marinade with a paper towel.
4. Grill or broil in a toaster oven until cooked through.

Misoyaki

This dish requires no time to marinate; it can be whipped up very quickly. *Miso* on its own is somewhat overpowering, so mayonnaise is used to make it a bit milder. This *miso* combination is very good with rice, too.

400 g fish fillets or a side of a fish (as long as it does not have bones, any fish is fine)
Miso paste (A)
    2 tablespoons *miso*
    2 tablespoons *mirin*
    2 tablespoons mayonnaise
    1 teaspoon soy sauce
3 stalks scallion
3 tablespoons minced fresh coriander

1. Finely chop scallions; mince coriander.
2. Combine *miso* paste ingredients; mix in scallions

菜もまぜる。

3 魚はグリルで片面を焼いて裏返し、もう片面は軽く焼く。皮がついている場合には皮の面を先に焼いておく。

4 身のほうに、味噌ダレを全体に塗りつける。

5 再びグリルに入れ、味噌にちょっと香ばしい焦げ目がつくまで焼く。

たたき

とびきり新鮮な刺身用の切り身が手に入ったときにどうぞ。焼き目の香ばしさと薬味の香りやオリーブオイルが味を補います。

生でも食べられる刺身用のサク
　（マグロ、カツオ、サケなど）……1切れ（200グラム程度）
タレ（A）
　醤油……………………………大さじ1
　レモン汁（ライム汁やすだち、柚子でも）……小さじ1
　わけぎ（小口切り）………大さじ3
　にんにく（すりおろして）…………小さじ½
　オリーブオイル…………大さじ1
　シソ（好みで）……………数枚を細く切る

1 テフロン加工のフライパンを熱し、魚の表面の色がすべて色が変わるように転がしながら焼きつける。

2 表面の色が変わったら、すぐに冷水にとって冷やす。冷めたらすぐに水から出してペーパータオルに包み、ラップでくるんで冷蔵庫で冷やしておく。

and coriander.
3. Grill one side of the fish; turn over. Grill the other side lightly. If the fish has skin on it, grill the side with skin first.
4. Fully coat the fleshy side with *miso* paste.
5. Grill again until the *miso* paste is lightly browned and fragrant.

Tataki (briefly seared fish)

You have to try this when you find some magnificently fresh sashimi-grade fish. Olive oil complements the fragrance of the seared fish and seasonings.

1 block sashimi-grade fish (tuna, bonito, salmon, etc.), about 200 g
Sauce (A)
   1 tablespoon soy sauce
   1 teaspoon lemon juice (or lime, *sudachi* [a Japanese green citrus], or *yuzu*)
   3 tablespoons chopped scallions
   ½ teaspoon grated garlic
   1 tablespoon olive oil
   Shiso (Japanese herb) a few leaves

1. Sear fish in a Teflon-coated frying pan, turning often, so that all surfaces are browned.
2. When the surfaces have browned, immerse in chilled water to cool. When cool, remove from water, wrap in paper towels, and wrap again with

3 食べる直前に食べやすい大きさに切り、(A)の材料をすべて合わせたタレを全体にかけ回し、わさびを添える。

天ぷら

天ぷらにはエビ、イカ、帆立(ほたて)のように、身がしっかりしているものが扱いやすいでしょう。コツは衣をまぜすぎないこと。衣が重くなってしまいます。そして、長く揚げすぎないこと。魚介類は短時間で火が通ります。肉類やフライドポテトは「きつね色になるまで揚げる」ことになっていますが、えびの天ぷらをキツネ色になるまで揚げたらエビは火が通りすぎてコチコチになってしまいます。

大きめのエビ……8匹
天ぷら粉…………½カップ
水 …………………½カップ
揚げ油……………適宜

＊天ぷら粉がない場合の衣のつくり方
　天ぷらは市販の天ぷら粉を使うのが一番簡単ですが、手に入らない場合は、次の配合でカラッと揚がります。小麦粉と片栗粉はあらかじめまぜてふるっておきます。

小麦粉……¼カップ
片栗粉……⅙カップ
よく冷えた炭酸水 …………⅓カップ

plastic wrap; refrigerate.
3. Slice in easy-to-eat pieces just before serving. Mix and pour on the sauce (A). Serve with wasabi on the side.

Tempura

Firm seafood, such as shrimp, squid, and scallops, is easy to use for tempura. The trick is to not over-mix the tempura batter; it will make the batter too heavy. Also, be careful not to over-fry the tempura. Seafood cooks through very quickly. Meat, potatoes, and such need to be deep fried until golden brown, but if you deep fry shrimp until golden brown they will become overcooked and stiff.

8 jumbo-size shrimp
½ cup tempura flour
½ cup water
Oil for deep frying

* Making tempura flour yourself
  It is easiest to use store-bought, ready-made tempura flour, but if that is not an option then prepare as follows for a nice, crispy batter. Combine and shift the flour and cornstarch in advance.

¼ cup flour
⅕ cup cornstarch
⅓ cup well-chilled soda water

1. エビは背ワタをとり、腹側のスジを数カ所切っておく。
2. 衣の材料を合わせます。このとき水を冷たくしておくこと（氷を1、2個入れるといい）。まぜすぎないよう注意。
3. 深めのフライパンか厚手の鍋に、サラダ油をたっぷり入れて熱する。衣を少し落とし、すぐに浮き上がってくるくらいになったら、エビに衣をつけて、油に入れる。一度にたくさん入れると油の温度が下がるので2匹程度にする。
4. エビはすぐに火が通るので、衣がカリッとなればできあがり。
5. ペーパータオルなどにのせて余分な油を切る。

①深めのフライパンか厚手の鍋にサラダ油をたっぷり入れ加熱する

②箸でかきまぜてから衣を少し落としてみる すぐに浮き上がったら適温

③エビに衣をつけ油に入れる 一度にたくさん入れると温度が下がるので2匹程度にする

1. Devein shrimp. Make several small horizontal slits on their undersides.
2. Mix batter ingredients; chill water well (you can add an ice cube or two). Mix, but do not over-mix.
3. Heat plenty of vegetable oil in a deep frying pan or a heavy saucepan. The oil is hot enough if a small amount of batter dropped in quickly rises to the surface. Coat shrimp with batter and deep-fry in batches of 2 to keep the temperature of the oil from going down too much.
4. The shrimp cook through very quickly, so if the batter is crisp, they are done.
5. Drain excess oil from shrimp on paper towels or absorbent paper.

---

1. Heat plenty of vegetable oil in a deep frying pan or a heavy saucepan.
2. Stir the hot oil with chopsticks then drop a bit of batter in. If it rises quickly, the oil is at the right temperature.
3. Coat the shrimp with batter and drop in the hot oil. Too many at the same time will lower the temperature of the oil, so fry them 2 at a time.

ホイル焼き

香りのある野菜やきのこなどと組み合わせるとおいしくなります。簡単にできて、後片づけも楽です。きのこ類はなくてもできますが、入れたほうがぐっと風味がよくなります。

魚の切り身（サケ、ヒラメ、タイなど）や帆立など
　好みの魚介類 ………………………………………… 4切れ
きのこ（えのきだけ、またはしいたけ） ………… 適宜
わけぎ、またはたまねぎ …………………………… 少々
バター ………… 大さじ2
レモン汁（ライム、柚子、すだち） ……………… 少々
塩

1. アルミホイルを魚の切り身1切れ（または好みの魚介類）をゆったりと包めるくらいの大きさに切って4つ用意する。
2. アルミホイルに魚の切り身を置き、塩を軽くふってレモン汁をしぼりかけ、きのこ類、わけぎ（3センチ程度に切る）またはたまねぎ（薄切り）少々を上にのせ、最後にバター大さじ½ずつをのせたら、全体を包むようにアルミホイルを閉じる。
3. 天板にホイル包みをのせ、摂氏200度（華氏400度）に温めたオーブンで火が通るまで焼く（約10分程度）。

Foil wraps

Fish grilled or baked in aluminum foil is great in combination with fragrant vegetables and mushrooms. These dishes are just as easy to clean up after as they are to prepare. They can be made without the mushrooms, but adding them really gives the dish a boost.

4 fish fillets (salmon, flounder, snapper, etc.) or other seafood, such as scallops
Mushrooms (*enoki*, *shiitake*, etc.), as desired
Scallions or onion, as needed
2 tablespoons butter
1 dash lemon juice (or lime, *sudachi* [a Japanese green citrus], or *yuzu*)
Salt

1. Prepare 4 sheets of aluminum foil, each large enough to loosely wrap a fish fillet (or other seafood).
2. Place a fish fillet in the center of the aluminum foil. Salt lightly; squeeze on some lemon juice. Add mushrooms and scallions (sliced in about 3-cm lengths) or thinly sliced onions. Top with ½ tablespoon butter; seal foil, repeat.
3. Bake on a baking sheet in a preheated oven at 200 C (400 F) until cooked through (about 10 minutes).

醤油や味噌で肉をおいしく

肉は日本料理の伝統的な素材ではありませんが、醤油や味噌がよく合います。照り焼きや唐揚げなどの定番肉料理は、子供から大人まで、みんなが大好きな味です。

照り焼き

アメリカの日本料理店のメニューでは欠かせない存在の照り焼き。甘辛醤油味の「照り焼きソース」なるものはスーパーでも手に入りますが、基本は砂糖と醤油の単純なものですから、家庭でも簡単につくれます。

肉類(鶏肉、牛肉、豚肉など、何でもOK)…… 400g
照り焼きダレ (A)
 醤油……………………………大さじ4
 砂糖……………………………大さじ2
 酒………………………………大さじ2
 バルサミコ酢 …………………小さじ1
 にんにくのすりおろし…小さじ1 (好みで)

1. (A)の材料をすべて合わせて照り焼きのタレをつくる。
2. 肉は焼きやすい厚さ (1センチ以下) にしておく。
3. タレに肉をつけ30分おく。
4. グリル、またはテフロン加工のフライパンで焼く。

Soy sauce and *miso* marinades for meat

Meat is not a traditional part of Japanese cuisine, but soy sauce and *miso* go nicely with it. Kids and adults alike enjoy the taste of dishes that are now standard, such as grilled teriyaki and fried chicken.

Teriyaki

Teriyaki dishes are a must on any Japanese restaurant menu in the United States. Salty yet sweet "teriyaki sauce" is available at supermarkets, but all it takes is some sugar and soy sauce, so it is very easy to make at home.

400 g meat (such as chicken, beef, or pork)
Teriyaki marinade (A)
  4 tablespoons soy sauce
  2 tablespoons sugar
  2 tablespoons sake
  1 teaspoon balsamic vinegar
  1 teaspoon grated garlic (optional)

1. Combine teriyaki marinade ingredients (A).
2. Slice meat thinly so that it is easy to grill (1-cm thick or less).
3. Marinade meat in the teriyaki mix for 30 minutes.
4. Grill or cook in a Teflon-coated frying pan. Teriyaki

焦げやすいので火加減に注意。
5 その間に肉を漬けたタレを小さな鍋に入れて火にかけ、ちょっととろみがつくくらいまで煮詰める。
6 焼き上がった肉に5をまぶしつけ、食べやすい大きさに切る。

＊秘密の隠し味

わかるかわからないかの微量でありながら、味をグレードアップさせる調味料の使い方を日本語で「隠し味」といいます。たとえば、この照り焼きのタレの隠し味はバルサミコ酢。少量なので酢の味はほとんど感じませんが、酢が入ることで味がぐっとしまるのです。そのほかにも、味をまろやかにするために甘味のない料理に少量の砂糖を加えることもよくあります。

焼き鳥

串刺しスタイルが定番ですが、竹串に刺した肉をグリルで焼くと串だけが焦げてしまうことが多いものです。焼き上がってから切り分けて串刺しにすると、ジューシーな上に簡単です。

鶏もも肉または胸肉（骨なし皮つき）……2枚
塩
焼き鳥のタレ（A）
　醤油……大さじ2
　砂糖……大さじ1

burns easily, so watch the heat.
5. While cooking the meat, simmer the leftover marinade in a small saucepan until it is reduced and thickened.
6. Coat the grilled meat with the thickened teriyaki sauce; slice into bite-size pieces.

* Secret "hidden flavorings"

A tiny amount of a seasoning which can hardly be noticed yet enhances a dish greatly is known in Japanese as kakushi-aji (hidden flavorings). For instance, in this teriyaki recipe, the hidden flavoring is the balsamic vinegar. Because only a small amount is used, the dish does not taste of vinegar, but the vinegar adds a certain sharpness to the dish. To make a dish milder, a pinch of sugar is often added to dishes that have no natural sweetness.

Yakitori

Though commonly skewered, the bamboo skewers frequently burn to a crisp on the grill before what is skewered is finished cooking. Grilling larger pieces first, then cutting and skewering them later is easier and makes for juicier *yakitori*.

2 chicken breasts or thighs (boneless, skin-on cuts)
Salt
Yakitori sauce (A)
    2 tablespoons soy sauce
    1 tablespoon sugar

酒………大さじ1
竹串………適宜

1 鶏肉には全体に軽く塩をふる。
〈塩味の場合〉
2 グリルで火が通るまでこんがり焼く。
〈タレ味の場合〉
2 (A)の材料をまぜて小鍋で煮立たせる。
3 グリルで肉を焼く。ほぼ火が通ったところでタレを塗り、さらにこんがりと焼く。

串に刺す場合は、どちらも焼き上がってから食べやすい大きさに切って、串に刺します。パーティーなどには、あらかじめつくっておいて、出す直前に電子レンジであたためます。

とんかつ

日本の肉の揚げ物の代表料理。衣になるパン粉はアメリカのブレッドクラムに比べて粒が大きいので、それだけ揚げ物のサクサク感が楽しめます。最近は英語名もそのままのpankoとして、アメリカの料理のレシピにも登場するようになっています。

豚肉（ロースまたはヒレ）……1センチ程度の厚さのもの500グラム
塩・こしょう………………少々
卵………1個

1 tablespoon sake
Bamboo skewers, as needed

1. Salt chicken thoroughly.

For salt flavor:

2. Grill until golden brown.

For sauce flavor:

2. In a small saucepan, bring *yakitori* sauce ingredients to a boil; turn down heat, simmer.
3. Grill chicken. When almost cooked through, coat with yakitori sauce; continue grilling until golden brown.

If serving the dish skewered, cut either style of chicken above into bite-size pieces and skewer them. For parties and other large groups they can be prepared in advance and heated in a microwave oven.

Tonkatsu (breaded, deep-fried pork cutlets)

This is Japan's most distinctive deep-fried meat dish. The bread crumbs used in Japan are larger than the bread crumbs used in the United States, so they are really crunchy when fried. These days you can find English recipes calling for "*panko*," the Japanese word for bread crumbs.

500 g pork (loin or tenderloin) sliced into 1-cm-thick cutlets
1 pinch each of salt and pepper
1 egg

小麦粉……¼カップ
パン粉……1カップ
揚げ油……適宜
ソース
からし（好みで）
キャベツ（つけあわせ）

1. 豚肉の両面に軽く塩こしょうをふる。
2. 卵をよく溶き、浅いボウルに入れる。
3. 深めの皿に小麦粉を入れる。
4. パン粉は大きめのボウルに入れる。
5. 豚肉に小麦粉をまぶし、余分な粉ははたいて落とし、卵にくぐらせる。
6. パン粉の入ったボウルに肉を入れて、全体にパン粉をよくまぶしつける。
7. 鍋か深めのフライパンに油をたっぷり入れ、火にかける。
8. 油にパン粉を落としてみて、すぐ浮き上がってくるくらいになったら適温。肉を入れる。
9. 途中で裏返し、パン粉がきつね色になるまでじっくり揚げる。
10. 食べやすい大きさに切り、千切りのキャベツと一緒に盛りつけて、ソースと芥子を添える。

＊キャベツの千切りとソース

とんかつにはキャベツの千切りがつきものです。ホットドッグにザワークラウト、ハンバーガーにフライドポテトなどと同じように、とんかつには千切りキャベツが必ずついてきます。キャベツには脂っこさを和らげて口を

¼ cup flour
1 cup panko (bread crumbs)
Oil for deep frying, as needed
Tonkatsu sauce
Mustard (optional)
Cabbage (accompaniment)

1. Season both sides of the pork steaks with salt and pepper.
2. Beat egg well; set aside in a shallow bowl.
3. Spread flour on a deep plate.
4. Put bread crumbs in a large bowl.
5. Toss pork cutlets in flour; shake off excess. Dip in beaten egg.
6. Place in bowl with bread crumbs; coat thoroughly.
7. Heat plenty of oil in a saucepan or deep frying pan.
8. The oil is at the right temperature if bread crumbs dropped in come right back to the surface. Add the pork.
9. Turn pork once halfway through cooking; continue deep-frying until golden brown.
10. Cut into easy-to-eat slices; place on serving plates with shredded cabbage. Serve with *tonkatsu* sauce and mustard.

* Shredded cabbage and *tonkatsu* sauce
   Tonkatsu always comes with shredded cabbage on the side. It is much like the sauerkraut that comes with a hot dog or the French fries that come with a hamburger—essential. The cabbage reduces the oiliness of

さっぱりさせる効果があるのです。キャベツの葉を千切りにするには、葉を洗ってから、1枚ずつロール状に丸めて切ると、きれいに細く仕上がります。

そして、キャベツとともにとんかつに欠かせないのがソース。日本では、市販品でさまざまな種類のものが出回っていますが、市販のソースが手元にない場合にはウスターソースとトマトケチャップをまぜて代用できます。ウスターソースもない場合には醤油にトマトケチャップをまぜてお試しください。辛いもの好きの方には、さらにタバスコを加えるのもおすすめです。

しょうが焼き

薄切り肉の代表的な食べ方。ごはんのおかずに最高です。

豚肉薄切り	400グラム
漬け汁（A）	
醤油	大さじ3
みりん	大さじ3
酒	大さじ1
しょうがのすりおろし	大さじ1
キャベツの千切り	お好きなだけ

1. キャベツはできるだけ細い千切りにして、皿に盛りつけておく。
2. (A)を合わせた漬け汁に肉を漬け込んで、10分から30分くらいおく。
3. テフロン加工のフライパンをよく熱してから肉を入

the dish and cleans the palate. To shred the cabbage, clean the leaves and roll each leaf tightly; slice thinly on the horizontal.

Along with the cabbage, *tonkatsu* has to have sauce. In Japan, you can buy many types of *tonkatsu* sauce at the supermarket, but if you cannot get hold of any, you can substitute a mix of Worcestershire sauce and tomato ketchup. And, if you cannot get hold of any Worcestershire sauce, you can substitute a mixture of soy sauce and tomato ketchup. For those of you who like a bit of spice, I suggest you try a little Tabasco mixed in.

Ginger pork

This is the classic way of preparing thinly sliced meat. It goes great with rice.

400 g thinly sliced pork
Marinade (A)
    3 tablespoons soy sauce
    3 tablespoons *mirin*
    1 tablespoon sake
    1 tablespoon grated ginger
Cabbage, thinly sliced, as you desire

1. Try to cut the cabbage as thinly as possible; arrange on serving dishes.
2. Marinate the pork in the marinade mixture (A) for 10 to 30 minutes.
3. Heat a Teflon-coated frying pan on high; when it

れ、炒める。肉にだいたい火が通ったら、漬け汁も加えさらに炒める。
4. キャベツの上に肉を肉汁ごと盛りつける。

つくね

丸く団子にしたものは、どういうわけか子供に好まれます。鶏肉でつくるつくねは牛肉のミートボールよりあっさりしています。

鶏ひき肉……………………400グラム
合わせ調味料（A）
　塩……………………小さじ¼
　酒……………………大さじ1
　醤油…………………小さじ1
　卵……………………1個
　片栗粉………………大さじ1
ねぎ（みじん切り）……大さじ3
煮汁（B）
　出汁…………………3カップ
　醤油…………………大さじ4
　みりん………………大さじ4（または砂糖大さじ2）

1. 合わせ調味料(A)の材料をよくまぜてから、ひき肉に加え、それにねぎを加えてさらにまぜる。
2. 鍋に煮汁(B)の材料を入れて煮立てる。
3. 煮立っている煮汁の中に、スプーンを2つ使って、

is very hot, add the pork, saute. When the pork is almost cooked through, add the leftover marinade; continue to saute.
4. Pour the meat and remaining cooking liquid over the cabbage.

Tsukune (Japanese chicken meatballs)

For some reason, ball-shaped food really appeal to kids. *Tsukune* made with chicken has a lighter taste than beef meatballs.

400 g ground chicken
Seasoning mixture (A)
    ¼ teaspoon salt
    1 tablespoon sake
    1 teaspoon soy sauce
    1 egg
    1 tablespoon cornstarch
3 tablespoons scallions (minced)
Cooking liquid (B)
    3 cups *dashi*
    4 tablespoons soy sauce
    4 tablespoons *mirin* or 2 tablespoons sugar

1. Mix seasonings (A) well. Add ground chicken and scallions; mix thoroughly.
2. Heat cooking liquid ingredients (B) in a saucepan; bring to a boil.
3. Form round meatballs out of the seasoned chicken

ひき肉を丸めて団子状にしたものを落としていく。

4. 煮汁は鶏団子がかぶるくらいの量にする。足りない場合は水を足して、煮汁が再び煮立ったら火を弱め、鶏団子に火が通るまで煮る(約20分)。火が通ったら、蓋をして、そのままおいて味をしみこませる。

エビ入りつくね

冷凍のエビを刻んで加えるだけで、つくねがグレードアップ。ぷりぷりした歯ごたえとちょっと複雑な味が楽しめます。

鶏ひき肉	400グラム
合わせ調味料（A）	
味噌	大さじ1
塩	小さじ1/2
砂糖	小さじ1
醤油	小さじ1
ねぎ（みじん切り）	大さじ3
エビ	100グラム

1. エビは殻と背ワタを取り、小さく刻んでおく。
2. 合わせ調味料（A）の材料を合わせてから鶏ひき肉とまぜ、よくまざったら刻んだエビを加えてさらにまぜる。
3. オーブンを摂氏200度（華氏400度くらい）に熱しておく。

mixture using 2 spoons; drop them into the boiling cooking liquid.
4. Make sure the cooking liquid just covers the meatballs. Add water if necessary; lower heat when the liquid returns to a boil and simmer meatballs until cooked through (about 20 minutes). When cooked through, turn off heat, cover, and let stand to absorb more flavor.

Tsukune (chicken meatball) with shrimp

The addition of chopped frozen shrimp to *tsukune* raises them to the next level. You can really enjoy their tender chewiness and complex blend of flavors.

400 g ground chicken
Seasoning mixture (A)
    1 tablespoon *miso*
    ½ teaspoon salt
    1 teaspoon sugar
    1 teaspoon soy sauce
    3 tablespoons scallions (minced)
100 g shrimp

1. Shell and devein shrimp; chop.
2. Combine seasoning ingredients (A). Mix in ground chicken; when it is thoroughly mixed, add chopped shrimp and combine.
3. Preheat oven to 200 C (400 F).

4 天板に、スプーンを2つ使って、鶏肉を直径3センチくらいの団子状にしたものを落としていく。

5 熱したオーブンで鶏団子を火が通るまで焼く（約10分）。串やナイフを刺して、流れる汁が透明になれば火が通ったということで、できあがり。

そぼろごはん

　子供からお年寄りまで幅広く好まれるごはんのおかず。卵とグリーンピースを組み合わせた3色そぼろごはんはお弁当の定番です。

〈そぼろ肉〉

鶏ひき肉……………………400グラム

合わせ調味料（A）

　醤油…………………………大さじ3

　砂糖…………………………大さじ1½

〈そぼろ卵〉

卵……………………………3個

砂糖…………………………大さじ1½

冷凍グリーンピース……少々

1 鍋に合わせ調味料（A）をすべて入れてよくまぜてから、ひき肉を加え、さらによくまぜる。

2 鍋を中火にかけ、菜箸か大ぶりのフォークでまぜながら、ゆっくりと火を通す。

3 鶏肉に火が通ったら、汁気がなくなるまでかきまぜながら、さらに煮る。

4. Form small meatballs (about 3-cm in diameter) using 2 spoons; lay them on a baking sheet.
5. Bake the meatballs in the preheated oven until cooked through (about 10 minutes). The meatballs are cooked through if the liquid from them runs clear after you poke them with a skewer or pierce them with the tip of a knife.

Ground chicken and egg with rice

This is considered a treat for people of all ages. The addition of egg and green peas makes this a 3-colored dish which has become standard in boxed lunches.

For the ground chicken
400 g ground chicken
Seasoning mix (A)
   3 tablespoons soy sauce
   1½ tablespoons sugar

For the egg mixture
3 eggs
1½ tablespoons sugar
1 handful of frozen green peas

1. Combine the seasoning ingredients (A) in a saucepan. Add ground chicken; mix again.
2. Heat saucepan on medium heat. Stir with chopsticks or a fork until slowly cooked through.
3. Continue cooking until the liquid has boiled off, stirring constantly.

4 別の鍋に卵と砂糖大さじ1½を入れ、よくまぜてから弱火にかける。
5 箸4本または大ぶりのフォークでまぜながら火を通す。
6 卵に火が通ってパラリとなったらできあがり。
7 白いごはんの上にそぼろ肉とそぼろ卵を色どりよくのせ、解凍したグリーンピースを散らす。

*そぼろ肉とそぼろ卵はただ並べるだけでなく、交互に並べて縞模様にしたり、クッキー型などを使って卵で形をつくったりすると、子供に喜ばれます。

唐揚げ

アメリカの日本料理店では「タツタアゲ」の名でメニューに載っています。鳥の唐揚げはもうずいぶん前から、日本の子供たちの人気家庭料理。衣に卵を入れることでやわらかく風味豊かに仕上がります。

鶏肉（もも肉でも胸肉でも好みで）‥‥600グラム
合わせ調味料（A）

 醤油‥‥‥‥‥‥‥‥‥‥‥‥‥ 大さじ3
 バルサミコ酢‥‥‥‥‥‥‥‥‥ 大さじ½
 にんにく（すりおろし）‥‥ 小さじ1
 砂糖‥‥‥‥‥‥‥‥‥‥‥‥‥ 小さじ1
卵 ‥‥‥‥‥‥‥‥‥‥‥‥‥‥‥‥‥ 1個
片栗粉‥‥‥‥‥‥‥‥‥‥‥‥‥‥‥ ½カップ
サラダ油

4. In a separate saucepan, combine the eggs and 1½ tablespoons of sugar; mix well and cook on low heat.
5. Using 4 chopsticks or an oversized fork, continue stirring while cooking.
6. The eggs are ready when they separate into small bits.
7. Top rice with chicken and egg so that the 2 colors are arranged in an appealing pattern; scatter thawed green peas on top.

* Using the 3 colors, make stripes or other patterns out of the toppings, or use cookie cutters as forms for different shapes; this is a treat for kids.

Japanese fried chicken

One item you can find on the menu at a Japanese restaurant in the United States is "*tatsuta-age*." Fried chicken has been a popular home-made item with Japanese kids for years and years. An egg added to the batter makes it softer and richer in flavor.

600 g chicken (thigh or breast)
Seasoning mixture (A)
    3 tablespoons soy sauce
    ½ tablespoon balsamic vinegar
    1 teaspoon grated garlic
    1 teaspoon sugar
1 egg
½ cup cornstarch
Vegetable oil

1. 鶏肉は食べやすい大きさに切り、(A)をまぜ合わせた調味料に30分ほど漬ける。
2. 溶いた卵と片栗粉を漬け汁ごと1に加えてまぜる。
3. 鍋か深めのフライパンにサラダ油をたっぷり入れて火にかける。
4. 衣を少し落としてみて、すぐに浮き上がってくるくらいになったら、肉を入れる。1回に入れる量は、重ならずに鍋の中で肉が動く程度。
5. きつね色になるまで中火でじっくりと揚げる。

やさしい味の卵料理

　甘い卵焼きは子供の好物ということになっていますが、大人にとってもお弁当にひと切れ入っているとうれしいもの。卵焼き器がなくてもテフロン加工のフライパンがあればきれいにできます。冷めてもおいしく、色もきれいなので、日本のお弁当には欠かせないアイテムになっています。

卵焼き

卵 ………… 3個
砂糖 ………… 大さじ1
醤油 ………… 小さじ¼
酒 ………… 小さじ1（なくても可）

1. Cut chicken into easily-eaten pieces; marinate in seasoning mixture (A) for about 30 minutes.
2. Beat egg. Add egg and cornstarch to marinated chicken mixture; mix and coat well.
3. Heat plenty of oil in a saucepan or deep frying pan.
4. Drop a small amount of batter into the oil; if it comes right back to the surface, the oil is hot enough. Add chicken to hot oil. Make sure you do not add too many pieces at the same time; they should have some space to float around between them.
5. Deep-fry on medium heat until golden brown.

A light and fluffy egg dish

It is said that kids love these sweet omelets, but even adults are happy to discover a slice or two in their boxed lunches. If you do not have the rectangular frying pan normally used for *tamago-yaki*, you can still make it in a Teflon-coated frying pan. It is attractive to the eye and delicious warm or cold, so it is a standard item in a Japanese boxed lunch.

Tamago-yaki (a Japanese-style omelet)

3 eggs
1 tablespoon sugar
¼ teaspoon soy sauce
1 teaspoon sake (optional)

サラダ油……少々

1. ボウルに卵を割り入れ、砂糖、醤油、酒を加えて、よくまぜる。
2. 長方形の卵焼き器か、普通の小さめのテフロン加工のフライパンを中火にかけて温める。
3. フライパンが熱くなったらサラダ油を入れ、ペーパータオルで全体にのばして余分な油をふき取る。油がしみたペーパータオルはお皿にとっておく。
4. フライパンに卵液の1/5程度を流し入れ、素早くフライパンを回して全体にのばす。
5. 卵が固まりかけたら、手前から向こうへ卵を巻いていく。
6. 手前の空いた部分を油のしみたペーパータオルでひとふきし、さらに同量の卵液を流し入れ素早く全体にのばす。
7. 今度は巻いた卵のある向こう側から手前に向かって卵を巻いていく。
8. これを卵液がなくなるまで繰り返す。
9. 最後にロール状になった卵を少し転がして、よく火を通してできあがり。

*箸の代用品

日本では、菜箸と呼ぶ料理用の大振りの箸を料理によく使います。使い慣れている日本人にとっては菜箸で料理するというのは当然なのですが、日常、箸を使い慣れない外国人にとっては箸で料理するなんて考えられないことです。そこで、外国人に日本料理を教える場合には、

1 dash vegetable oil (as needed)

1. Combine eggs, sugar, soy sauce, and sake in a bowl; mix well.
2. Heat a rectangular *tamago-yaki* pan or small Teflon-coated frying pan on medium heat.
3. Add oil when pan is hot; use a paper towel to coat the entire surface with a thin coating of oil, removing the excess. Reserve the oily paper towel.
4. Pour about 1/5 of the egg mixture into the pan and cook, quickly tilting the pan from side to side to spread the mixture evenly.
5. When the egg mixture becomes firm, roll from front to back.
6. Brush the exposed area in front of the omelet lightly with the oil-soaked paper towel. Add another 1/5 of the egg mixture, quickly tilting the pan to spread it evenly.
7. This time, roll from the back to the front.
8. Continue this process until the egg mixture is used up.
9. When the roll is completed, turn the entire roll over and cook through.

* Chopstick substitutes
In Japan, oversized chopsticks are often used for cooking and serving food. For Japanese, who are used to using these, they are a perfectly normal kitchen utensil, but for many foreigners, who are not used to using them, their use is entirely unthinkable.

菜箸の代用品が必要になります。

実際にやってみると、その料理によって代用品もさまざまで、箸がいかに万能かよくわかります。肉や魚をつかむにはトングが一番です。卵をかきまぜたりするのにはフォーク。炒め物はヘラで。そして、一番困るのがこの卵焼きなのですが、ケーキをデコレーションしたりするときに使うスパチュラの小さいものが使いやすいようです。薄焼き卵を裏返したりするのにもこれを使います。

①肉や魚にトング
②フォークで卵をほぐす
③卵焼きにスパチュラ
④炒めものにはヘラ

親子どんぶり

卵と鶏肉で親子どんぶりとはよく考えれば妙な名前です。鶏肉を牛肉や豚肉にかえると他人丼と呼ばれたりします。名前に似合わず、誰にでも好まれるやさしい味です。

鶏胸肉……………………200グラム

Therefore, when teaching foreigners how to cook Japanese food, you need a substitute for these chopsticks.

There are plenty of substitutes for a given type of cooking, but you soon realize how useful cooking chopsticks really are. For grasping meat and fish, tongs work best. Forks are okay for beating eggs and such. For sauteing and stir-frying, a wooden spatula can be used. But finding a substitute for chopsticks is most difficult when making *tamago-yaki*. The best utensil to use in this case is the small frosting spatulas often used for decorating cakes. These are also useful when making crepe-like fried eggs.

---

1. Use thongs for meat and fish.
2. Use a fork to beat eggs.
3. Use a frosting spatula for *tamago-yaki*.
4. Use a wooden spatula for stir-frying.

Oyako donburi (chicken and egg on rice)

When you think about it, *oyako donburi* is a strange name for a chicken and egg mixture on rice ("*oya*" means parent and "*ko*" means child). When pork or beef is substituted for the chicken, it becomes "*tanin-don*" ("*tanin*" means "unrelated person"). Naming aside, everybody loves the taste.

200 g chicken breasts

たまねぎ（薄切り）…½個
卵………………………4個（溶いておく）
煮汁（A）
　出汁…………………1カップ
　醤油（しょうゆ）……………大さじ1
　みりん………………大さじ3
　塩……………………小さじ½

1. 鶏肉はひと口大のそぎ切り、たまねぎは薄切りにしておく。
2. 煮汁（A）を深めのフライパンで煮立て、たまねぎを入れる。
3. 再び煮立ったら鶏肉を加え、中火で火が通るまで煮る（約3〜5分）。
4. よく溶いた卵を回し入れる。
5. ざっとかきまわして火を通し、すぐに火を止める。卵を入れたら煮すぎないのがコツ。
6. 煮汁ごと丼に盛ったごはんにかける。

½ onion (thinly sliced)
4 eggs (beaten)
Cooking liquid (A)
- 1 cup *dashi*
- 1 tablespoon soy sauce
- 3 tablespoons *mirin*
- ½ teaspoon salt

1. Cut chicken into bite-size pieces; thinly slice onion.
2. Bring cooking liquid (A) to a boil in a deep saucepan; add onion.
3. When liquid returns to a boil, add chicken; simmer on medium heat until cooked through (3 to 5 minutes).
4. Stir in well-beaten egg.
5. Keep stirring until just cooked through; turn off heat. The trick is not overcooking the egg.
6. Pour mixture (including cooking liquid) over big bowls of rice.

7

便利な調味料やスパイスの使い方
Convenient Seasonings
—How to Use Them

日本料理といえるものをつくるのに最低限必要な調味料は、醬油。ほかに代用がきかないものといえば味噌でしょう。あればバリエーションが広がるのが、みりん、かつお節や昆布、海苔など。そのほか、だしのもとやめんつゆ、ポン酢、すし酢は、冷蔵庫にあるととても便利です。

醬油

　いまや醬油はアメリカのスーパーマーケットでも置いてないところはないほど当たり前の調味料になりました。ただし薄口醬油、有機醬油など、種類もブランドもさまざまに出そろっている日本のようにはいきません。そんな中で、日本よりもなぜかよく見かけるのが、減塩醬油とたまり醬油です。

　特に減塩醬油は、アメリカのスーパーや日本食レストランに必ずといっていいほど置かれていますが、減塩にしたければ塩や醬油の量を減らせばいいだけなので、特に必要ありません。この減塩醬油はlight soy sauceとして売られているので、薄口醬油と誤解される場合もありますが、まったく別物です。薄口醬油は色こそ薄いものの、塩分は普通の醬油（濃い口）より多く含まれています。素材の色を生かして仕上げたいときや、あっさりとした味に仕上げたいときに用いますが、醬油を少なくして塩を補うことで代用できます。

At the very least, you need soy sauce when making Japanese food. There is also no substitute for *miso*. *Mirin*, bonito flakes, *konbu*, and *nori*, if available, allow you to broaden your cooking experience. In addition to these, keeping some instant *dashi*, noodle broth, *ponzu* (a sauce made mainly from soy sauce and citrus juice), and sushi vinegar in the refrigerator can be very helpful.

Soy sauce

Soy sauce has become so common, it is impossible to find a supermarket in the United States that does not carry any. But you still do not see the variety of *usukuchi* soy sauces, organic soy sauces, and others that you find in Japan. It is surprising, too, when you see so much more low-salt soy sauce and *tamari* soy sauce in the United States than in Japan.

In particular, low-salt soy sauce is common in the United States, at supermarkets and restaurants, but you can just use less salt and soy sauce if you want to cut your salt intake. Low-salt soy sauce is sometimes sold as "light soy sauce," so please do not confuse it with *usukuchi* (light, in color) soy sauce. They are completely different. "Light" soy sauce actually contains more salt than standard soy sauce (*koikuchi*). *Usukuchi* (light color) soy sauce can be used to highlight the natural colors of ingredients or to give a dish a lighter taste, but

たまり醤油は、アメリカの自然食品ストアにかなり以前から並んでいます。日本では一部の地方を除いて、たまり醤油を常備している家庭は少ないと思いますが、どういうわけか自然食志向の一部のアメリカ人の間ではよく知られています。中には「たまり醤油は普通の醤油よりナチュラルである」と思い込んでいる人もいて驚かされます。醤油は同量の大豆と小麦を醗酵させてつくりますが、その小麦の割合がごくわずかなのがたまり醤油です。濃い口醤油よりさらに色も味も濃厚になります。

味噌

醤油に比べると味噌は、まだ海外では一般的とはいえませんが、アジア食材店でなくとも自然食品店で扱っているところがかなりあります。

味噌はブランドや種類によって塩味も甘みも風味もさまざまで、一般的にいって色が濃いほど味噌風味が濃厚になります。中でも、特に白っぽい西京味噌は「白味噌」とも呼ばれ、かなり甘みの強い特殊な味噌です。また、逆に黒っぽい八丁味噌は「赤味噌」とも呼ばれ、これも通常の味噌とは用途も味わいも異なる味噌です。レシピに「味噌」とだけある場合には、西京味噌や八丁味噌は使いません。味噌の種類は見た目だけでは判断できない

you can achieve the same results by using less ordinary soy sauce and adding a bit of salt.

Tamari soy sauce has been on the shelves of health food stores in the United States for quite some time. I doubt that *tamari* soy sauce is a regularly stocked item in most Japanese kitchens, except for in some particular region of Japan, but for some reason it appears to be quite well known among some American health food enthusiasts. Some have claimed, very surprisingly, that *tamari* soy sauce is more natural than ordinary soy sauce. Ordinary soy sauce uses roughly equal amounts of soy and wheat, but *tamari* soy sauce uses very little. It is darker and richer in flavor than standard *koikuchi* soy sauce.

Miso

Compared with soy sauce, *miso* is still not widely available overseas, but you can usually find it in health food stores without going to Asian food stores.

Although there are many varieties and brands of *miso* with rich flavors ranging from salty to sweet, in general, the darker the *miso* the richer the taste. Among the many varieties of *miso*, *saikyo miso*, also known as "white *miso*," is lightest in color; it has a particular sweet taste all its own. In contrast, *hatcho miso*, also known as "red *miso*," is darker in color; its taste and use also differ from ordinary *miso*. When a recipe calls for "*miso*" only,

ので、ラベルを読むことが必要ですが、日本語が読めない場合には、店頭にある味噌から中間くらいの色合いのものを選ぶのが無難です。

保存は冷蔵庫で。もともとが保存食ですから簡単に腐るものではありませんが、封を切ったあと長くおけば風味は落ちます。

7 酒

日本料理では酒をよく使います。煮込む過程でアルコール分はとんでしまいますが、風味を増したり、やわらく仕上げたり、味をよくしみさせたりと、さまざまな作用があるからです。あまり高価でない酒を料理用に常備しておき、料理に気軽に使えるようにしておくことをおすすめします。

酒は一升瓶（約1.8ℓ）または5号瓶（約900㎖）が一般的ですが、牛乳パックのようなカートン入り（約900㎖）もあります。ワインのように、あけたあとすぐ飲みきらなければならないわけではありませんが、涼しいところに保存してなるべく早く使い切るようにします。

なお、「料理酒」として販売されているものは塩分が含まれているので飲用には向きません。料理に使用するときも味つけに注意が必要です。

do not use either of these. You cannot really be certain about *miso* just by looking at it on the shelf; you should read the label, but if you cannot read Japanese, you are best off choosing one in the middle of the color range available.

Miso should be kept in the refrigerator. Since *miso* is originally a preserved food, you do not need to worry about it going off, but it will lose some of its flavor if left out for long periods of time after opening.

Sake

Sake is used in a lot of Japanese dishes. A bit of simmering will evaporate off the alcohol, but it also has the added effect of softening foods, and increasing and concentrating their flavors. I recommend keeping a not-so-expensive bottle of sake in the cupboard and using it freely whenever a recipe calls for it.

Sake is usually sold in 1.8 ℓ bottles and 900 mℓ bottles, but you can also find it in 900 mℓ cartons. After opening, you do not need to use it up very quickly as you do with wine, but it is best to store it in a cool place and use it up as quickly as possible.

What is sold as "cooking sake" has salt added to it, so it is not suitable for drinking. When used in cooking, adjust your seasonings accordingly.

みりん

　みりんは甘味料として用いられる甘味の強い酒です。砂糖よりも甘さが穏やかで、料理に風味を加えたり、つやを出すはたらきもあります。液体なので和え物などに使うにも重宝します。煮物、めんつゆ、照り焼きなど、和風味の基本は醤油とみりんがだいたい1対1と覚えておいてください。これを基礎に、料理の種類や好みによって、醤油、塩、砂糖、みりんで味を調節します。

だしのもと・めんつゆ

　かつおや、昆布、煮干しの和風の出汁を顆粒状にしたのがだしのもと。必要に応じて水やお湯に溶かして使います。

　出汁に醤油やみりん、砂糖で味つけしたのがめんつゆです。めんつゆはその名のとおり、麺類のつゆですが、ほかにも煮物や和え物などに便利に使えます。製品により2倍や4倍の濃縮になっていますから、味をみながら好みの濃さに水で薄めて使います。濃縮のものをそのまま調味料として用いれば、日本料理らしい味が手軽に楽しめます。

Mirin

Mirin is a very sweet type of sake used for sweetening dishes. Its sweetness is gentler than sugar, and it adds flavor and luster. Since it is a liquid, it is particularly appreciated as an ingredient in dressings. For a true Japanese taste in simmered dishes, noodle broths, and teriyaki dishes, just remember to use 1 part *mirin* to 1 part soy sauce—this is fundamental. With that understood, you can adjust the amounts of soy sauce, salt, sugar and *mirin* to the type of dish and your personal preference.

Instant *dashi* (soup stock) granules and noodle broths

Instant *dashi* is granulated *dashi,* which is made from bonito flakes, *konbu*, dried sardines, and such. It can be dissolved as needed in cold or hot water.

When soy sauce, *mirin*, sugar, and other seasonings are added to *dashi*, it becomes noodle broth (*men-tsuyu*). *Men-tsuyu* literally means "noodle broth," or a sauce for dipping noodles into, but it has a variety of uses, such as in simmered dishes and dressings. It is usually sold concentrated 2 to 4 times, so taste as you dilute with water to get the concentration you want. If you use it

だしのもともめんつゆもインスタント食品の１つですが、日本の大多数の家庭で常備されているアイテムです。アメリカでいえば、スープキューブや缶詰のスープストックにあたるようなもの。そのものを味わうというより、料理の中に利用すると便利です。

　めんつゆは開封後は冷蔵庫で保存します。濃縮のものでも醬油などの調味料のように長持ちするわけではないので、なるべく小型のものを購入して早く使い切るようにします。だしのもとは顆粒ですから、そう簡単にいたむことはありませんが、封を切ったあとは、時間とともに風味が落ちます。

海藻類

　海苔も、昆布も、わかめも、英語でいうと、すべてシーウィードになってしまいますが、海草類の中で外国人にもとりわけなじまれているのが、寿司でおなじみの海苔。レシピにシーウィードと書いてあったからと、酢飯を炊くのに昆布を入れるべきところに海苔を入れて炊いて真っ黒なごはんができたという話も聞きます。英語にするときはシーウィードでくくらずに、海苔はnori、昆布はkonbu、と日本語そのままで説明したほうが親切です。

as is as a seasoning for other foods, you can easily get a distinctly Japanese taste.

Dashi granules and noodle-broth are both instant, and are items found regularly in a Japanese home's kitchen. These equate to the bouillon cubes and canned soup stocks found in home kitchens in the United States. They are not meant to be enjoyed on their own, but rather to be conveniently used when cooking.

Noodle broth should be refrigerated after opening. Even though it is concentrated, it does not keep well as soy sauce and other seasonings do, so you are better off buying small bottles and using them up quickly. Instant *dashi* does not go bad easily, but once opened it will lose flavor over time.

Seaweed

Nori, *konbu*, and *wakame* are all "seaweed" in English, but the one type of seaweed that foreigners can easily recognize and are familiar with is the *nori* they see wrapped around sushi rolls. I have heard of sushi rice recipes calling for the addition of "seaweed" when cooking the rice—*nori* was added instead of *konbu*, resulting in dark black rice. It is more helpful to teach foreigners that *nori* is *nori*, *konbu* is *konbu*.

かつお節

出汁をとるのに欠かせないほか、おひたしやサラダのトッピングにしたり、煮物や炒め物に加えたりと、日本料理らしい風味を加えるのに便利な調味料です。本来、かつお節はかつおの切り身を蒸して乾燥させたもので、その名のとおり節（かたまり）になっているのをカンナのようなかつお節削りで使うたびに削って使うものでした。現在では、日本国内でもかつお節削りのある家庭は少数派で、海外では丸ごとのかつお節は手に入れることも困難でしょう。

ほとんどの家庭で常備されているのは、すでに削ってパックに入っている削り節です。削り節は封を切るとすぐに生臭さが出てくるので、よほど大量に出汁をとるのでないかぎり、5グラム以下の袋に小分けになったものを購入するのをおすすめします。

ポン酢

柚子やすだちなど、日本の柑橘類の絞り汁に醤油、みりん、昆布出汁などを加えたものがポン酢です。鍋をはじめ、野菜のドレッシング代わりにも使えます。また、ポン酢と大根おろし、あるいはポン酢とわさびをつけると、焼いただけの魚や肉が驚くほどおいしく食べられます。

Dried bonito flakes

Bonito flakes are essential for making *dashi*, but they are also used as a topping for *ohitashi* and salads, added to simmered and sauteed dishes, and are convenient to add a bit of Japanese flavor to other dishes, as well. As the name in Japanese implies, bonito flakes were originally shaved off a dried piece of bonito with a special utensil each time they were needed. There are very few kitchens even in Japan these days that have the special bonito planers that were originally used, and finding lumps of dried bonito overseas is next to impossible.

Almost all Japanese have packaged, shaved bonito flakes in their kitchens. The flakes begin to take on a fishy smell not long after opening the bag, so, unless you are planning on making *dashi* for a small army, buy packages that have smaller, 5 g packages of bonito flakes inside.

Ponzu

Ponzu is made from Japanese citrus juices, such as *yuzu* and *sudachi*, combined with soy sauce, mirin, and *konbu dashi*. Commonly used as a dipping sauce for one-pot dishes, it can also be used as a substitute for vegetable dressings. It is also surprising how much more

すし酢

炊きたてのごはんにまぜるだけで酢飯ができます。米酢に塩、砂糖、昆布出汁などが入ったもので、酢飯のほかにも酢の物やサラダドレッシングなどに利用すると便利です。私は、アメリカに住むようになって寿司の登場回数が増え、すし酢が手放せなくなりました。

わさび

わさびも寿司でおなじみです。生のわさびをおろしたものが最も上等なのはいうまでもありませんが、常備するわけにはいきませんし、海外では望むべくもないものです。そこでチューブ入りか粉わさびとなります。めったに使わないなら粉、しょっちゅう使うならチューブですが、初めて寿司に挑戦する外国人には、価格からも保存性のよさからも粉をおすすめします。

delicious grilled fish and meats taste with a *ponzu* and grated *daikon* sauce, or a *ponzu* and wasabi sauce.

Sushi vinegar

Sprinkling sushi vinegar over freshly cooked rice and folding it in is enough to make sushi rice. A combination of rice vinegar, salt, sugar, *konbu dashi*, and other ingredients, sushi vinegar has many convenient uses, such as in salad dressings and vinegared vegetables. Since coming to the United States, I have had to make sushi more and more frequently, so I must be careful to never run out of sushi vinegar.

Wasabi

Wasabi is well known thanks to its relationship with sushi. Grated fresh wasabi root is ideal, of course, but it cannot always be kept on hand; you cannot expect to find it overseas. Here is where the wasabi-in-the-tube or powdered wasabi come to the rescue. If you rarely use wasabi, get the powdered version, but if you use it fairly frequently, I suggest the wasabi in tubes. But, for beginning sushi makers overseas, I suggest using the powdered version for its lower cost and non-perishable qualities.

日本の野菜

しそ

香りのよい日本のハーブで、生の葉を使います。刻んで料理に入れるほか、葉の形のまま料理のあしらいにすることもよくあります。緑の青じそと濃い赤紫色の赤じそがありますが、料理に使われるのは主に青じそです。さわやかな香りなので夏の料理に活躍します。また魚料理に使うと生臭みを抑えることができます。日本では1年中どこでも安価に出回っています。アメリカでも日本食料品店で入手できます。またバジルやパセリなどのハーブと同様、庭先やプランターで簡単に栽培もできます。

ねぎ、わけぎ

日本には、数多くの種類のネギが出回っています。あさつきのように細く緑のものから、東京ねぎや下仁田ねぎのように太くて白いものまであります。本来は用途に合わせて使い分けますが、ほとんどのレシピはアメリカのどこのスーパーマーケットにもあるスカリオンと呼ばれる中間タイプのネギで代用できます。日本で出回っているネギ各種の一般的な英語名は存在しないので、本書では長ネギタイプのネギ類の英訳はすべてscallionとしました。

Japanese Vegetables

Shiso (Japanese mint)

A Japanese herb with a pleasant aroma, it is used raw—not only sliced finely with food, but also decoratively as a whole leaf. There are two types, the green *aojiso* and the red *akajiso*, but it is the green *shiso* that is commonly used. With its refreshing aroma, it is popularly used with summer dishes. It also lessens the fishy smell associated with fish dishes. It is available year-round all over Japan at reasonable prices. It is available in the United States, too, at Japanese food stores. Or, as with basil and parsley, you can grow it easily at home in your garden or in planters.

Negi and *Wakegi*

There are numerous varieties of *negi* (Japanese leeks) available in Japan. They range from the thin, green type similar to chives, to the thick, white types such as Tokyo *negi* and Shimonita negi. Normally, types of *negi* should be chosen according to its intended use, but in the United States you can use ordinary scallions (somewhere in between) which are available in supermarkets everywhere. There are no common English terms for the types of *negi* used in Japan, so in this book "scallion" is used as a translation for the long type of *negi* commonly used.

E-CAT

English **C**onversational **A**bility **T**est
国際英語会話能力検定

● E-CATとは…
英語が話せるようになるための
テストです。インターネット
ベースで、30分であなたの発
話力をチェックします。

www.ecatexam.com

iTEP

● iTEP®とは…
世界各国の企業、政府機関、アメリカの大学300校以上が、英語能力判定テストとして採用。オンラインによる90分のテストで文法、リーディング、リスニング、ライティング、スピーキングの5技能をスコア化。iTEP®は、留学、就職、海外赴任などに必要な、世界に通用する英語力を総合的に評価する画期的なテストです。

www.itepexamjapan.com

[対訳ニッポン双書]
日本の料理
Japanese Cooking for Everyone

2009年9月11日　第1刷発行
2024年9月6日　第6刷発行

著　者　　黒田　基子
訳　者　　リチャード・モン

発行者　　賀川　　洋

発行所　　IBCパブリッシング株式会社
　　　　　〒162-0804 東京都新宿区中里町29番3号 菱秀神楽坂ビル
　　　　　Tel. 03-3513-4511　Fax. 03-3513-4512
　　　　　www.ibcpub.co.jp

印刷所　　株式会社シナノパブリッシングプレス

© 黒田基子 2009
© IBC Publishing, Inc. 2009

Printed in Japan

落丁本・乱丁本は、小社宛にお送りください。送料小社負担にてお取り替えいたします。
本書の無断複写（コピー）は著作権法上での例外を除き禁じられています。

ISBN978-4-7946-0015-8